ESCAPING

THE GROWTH CURSE

ESCAPING

THE GROWTH CURSE

The Path to Stronger Corporate Strategy

Yves Doz and Keeley Wilson

Berrett–Koehler Publishers, Inc.

Berrett-Koehler Publishers, Inc.
1333 Broadway, Suite 1000
Oakland, CA 94612–1921
Tel: (510) 817–2277
Fax: (510) 817–2278
www.bkconnection.com

ORDERING INFORMATION

Quantity sales. Special discounts are available on quantity purchases by corporations, associations, and others. For details, contact the "Special Sales Department" at the Berrett-Koehler address above.
Individual sales. Berrett-Koehler publications are available through most bookstores. They can also be ordered directly from Berrett-Koehler: Tel: (800) 929–2929; Fax: (802) 864–7626; www.bkconnection.com.
Orders for college textbook/course adoption use. Please contact Berrett-Koehler: Tel: (800) 929–2929; Fax: (802) 864–7626.

Distributed to the U.S. trade and internationally by Penguin Random House Publisher Services.

Berrett-Koehler and the BK logo are registered trademarks of Berrett-Koehler Publishers, Inc.

Printed in the United States of America

Berrett-Koehler books are printed on long-lasting acid-free paper. When it is available, we choose paper that has been manufactured by environmentally responsible processes. These may include using trees grown in sustainable forests, incorporating recycled paper, minimizing chlorine in bleaching, or recycling the energy produced at the paper mill.

Library of Congress Cataloging-in-Publication Data

Names: Doz, Yves L., author. | Wilson, Keeley, author.
Title: Escaping the growth curse : the path to stronger corporate strategy / Yves Doz and Keeley Wilson.
Description: First edition. | Oakland, CA : Berrett-Koehler Publishers, Inc., [2024] | Includes bibliographical references and index.
Identifiers: LCCN 2023049973 (print) | LCCN 2023049974 (ebook) | ISBN 9781523087259 (hardcover) | ISBN 9781523087266 (pdf) | ISBN 9781523087273 (epub)
Subjects: LCSH: Sustainable development. | Economic development. | Business planning.
Classification: LCC HC79.E5 D699 2024 (print) | LCC HC79.E5 (ebook) | DDC 338.9/27—dc23/eng/20240216
LC record available at https://lccn.loc.gov/2023049973
LC ebook record available at https://lccn.loc.gov/2023049974

First Edition

32 31 30 29 28 27 26 25 24   10 9 8 7 6 5 4 3 2 1

Book producer: Westchester Publishing Services
Cover designer: Adrian Morgan

Contents

PART THREE. Making Strategy Stronger ■ 155

There is no doubt in my mind, after three decades of working with chairs, CEOs, and boards, that we need to unlock more of the potential of our boards around the world. Yves and Keeley call for a new blueprint for more effective and strategic boards. Chasing profit growth and being chased on governance regulation doesn't necessarily make for sustainable boards and employers that are fit for the future. We need more strategic, self-aware, and curious boards with higher levels of consciousness and societal responsibility. Yves and Keeley dig into the issues with great candor and stark analysis. They invite us to consider a different framing for boards and offer practical insights on what it's going to take. Boards are much-needed "meaning makers" or "conscience keepers," as Keeley and Yves call them. We need them on the balcony, taking on a more expansive identity with more strategic foresight and, to be frank, adding more value. To do that, boards need to elevate and modulate; they need the courage to reimagine their role and purpose. This book compellingly invites us to spark the collective imagination of boards. It is a "must read" to unlock the potential of boards whatever their sector, footprint, or even ownership. While it shines a light on the "illusion of growth" in public markets, I'd say many of its lessons are transversal for boards.

On first reading, I empathized with those CEOs discussed in the early chapters who are highlighted for their failures. The analysis is tough and revealing. Yet, I also came to see that Yves and Keeley are pointing to the inevitability of disappointing investors. Given the conflicting demands made of CEOs, Yves and Keeley are in fact acknowledging the "mission impossible" given to CEOs, and they are helping us to see an alternative way of viewing stewardship and governance evolution.

I've witnessed CEOs who go through the motions with their boards, and I've seen others who really leverage their board to enrich their thinking. The latter tend to share what they are wrestling with. They focus on the polarities and ethical dilemmas and go deep into what triggers them, what excites them—their sources of hope and fears. All of that requires psychological safety and "holding" in the boardroom. If you try and discuss such topics when the board is flying too low, it's seen as weakness. But if boards elevate and fly at a strategic "altitude," they get to the exploratory space where new insights are more likely to emerge. We need boards that resemble the wisdom councils of old times: wisdom seekers who create a whole that is greater than the sum of the parts. It's great to hear Yves and Keeley calling for boards to take their full space as curious custodians of strategy, not just rubber-stamping strategic plans that all too often have a time horizon that, coincidentally, reflects the CEO's anticipated tenure. Then what? We need more strategic imagination from boards in their stewardship.

This book explores the economic pressures and short-term circularity that too often limit the imagination of CEOs and boards. Public market expectations make our quoted company boards captive to quarterly reporting and proven growth outlooks. Indeed, we do need our boards to retain a healthy degree of achievement drive and to have growth mindsets, but they need to be balanced, sustainable, and strategically grounded. This special book goes further. It's not just a study on the impact of the "growth curse," but it also probes who is sitting around the table making these decisions and what motivates these individuals to join boards in the first place. To me, the old phrase "servant leadership" is relevant, with the emphasis on both the "serving" and the "leadership." Grandiosity, CV building, and identity preservation are not the motivations we need around the board table when facing such burning planetary and social issues as we now so clearly do. Yves and Keeley walk us through the traits needed in the people who are our strategic custodians on boards.

A year ago, when I stepped down from the role of chairwoman of Egon Zehnder (EZ), a global leadership firm, I had a strong calling to leverage all my "learning on the job" and from decades of advising boards to help other chairs and boards unlock more of their potential. We already had a fabulous board retreat, which we run with the University of St. Gallen, focusing on knowledge, skills, and tradecraft for board members. I had cofounded a CEO development program run by EZ and its partner, Mobius, a decade ago as well. But I still had a sense that chairs were being underserved when it came to leadership development. Why does our personal development stop when we join boards or become chairs? So, we set up a three-day program on "Chairing Boards from Within," to engage in deep development work, where cohorts of international chairs explore purpose, identity, motivations, and patterns, both their own and those of their boards. We look at board constellations and together create wider horizons and deeper development commitments. If I had read this book earlier, I might have arrived at this point sooner! It should certainly be preparatory, thought-provoking reading for our participants. I regard this book as an invitation to play our collective part in helping to transform boards in an era of great complexity and significance. Unlocking more of the potential of our boards and organizations is an imperative. Rather than retiring from Egon Zehnder after chairing it, I feel as though I've chosen it for the second time in my life because the mission to help transform boards is so clear. Having peers like Yves and Keeley stepping up with such a clear ask of our boards is both inspiring and reassuring. Governance is certainly important, but it needs to be set in a more developmental journey for boards to pursue. Here is the blueprint.

Allow me to focus on culture and the role boards should play in that context. We've seen too many situations where a board's awareness and antennae on culture have been dormant. The implicit contract with employees and society appears to have changed; what got us here is no longer sufficient. In fact, it's a risk that most boards are not reflecting in their risk registers. Today, boards have a responsibility to gauge the resonance and relevance of the organization's values, the degree to which leadership "walks the talk" on culture, and how up-to-date their grievance procedures are—or, more pertinently, their reactions and responses to grievances. That's no longer just an executive responsibility. We are seeing many countries in which cultural stewardship by boards is needed and expected. Let's raise our game on culture along with our curiosity and concern for such matters.

I was pleased to see Yves and Keeley cover this issue.

Board effectiveness reviews have become core to good governance and transparency. There's definite progress. Yet I realized we are asking questions that are too narrowly defined. I now approach board reviews through a constellation lens, looking for what is in flow or out of kilter, helping boards to be more curious and self-aware, fostering discussions about their patterns, which in itself starts to shift them. Yves and Keeley provide a highly relevant lens on board evolution and a mirror to help us see where we've become stuck and how to be more in synch with what's needed from boards in the future. I'm grateful to them.

Leading from the board in this level of complexity requires us to be sensing, to understand our patterns as a board, to work within the broader ecosystem, and to always be curious. Those things might not feel "leaderly" and "board-like"; they certainly go way beyond compliance. But more of the same won't cut it. We need fit-for-the future boards, and Keeley and Yves provide us with very helpful frameworks and reflective questions to gauge our boards' strategic agility or rigidity, our external antennae, and our internal congruence. This book is essential reading for board members who want to make a difference at a board-appropriate "altitude." Well done, Yves and Keeley!

Dame Jill Ader, senior adviser and former chairwoman, Egon Zehnder

ESCAPING

THE GROWTH CURSE

Introduction

Escaping the Growth Curse

Over the past four decades, the growth curse has become a pervasive problem for the companies ensnared by it, the people whose lives are made miserable by it, and the societies that ultimately suffer as a result of it. So, what is the curse at the heart of this book?

In short, as companies mature, their underlying growth naturally slows. Yet investors have come to expect continual strong growth. To meet these demands, chief executive officers (CEOs) and senior executives buckle under pressure and focus on delivering short-term financial results—or the "illusion of growth." But this type of growth comes at a devastating cost. It's a distraction from developing genuine value-creating strategies. It weakens the company, making it less resilient in the face of disruption and inflection points. And ironically, it hastens a firm's decline by directing resources and energy to shoring up the illusion of growth instead of building capabilities to redirect the company toward new challenges.

From investors to individuals, we have come to expect the increasing returns and improved lifestyles made possible by continual short-term corporate growth. But this endless pursuit of growth, with its handful of winners but many more losers, is folly and unsustainable. In the face of environmental degradation, growing complexity, and increasing volatility (from pandemics to mass migration and terrorism to political populism), we need to find a new model of corporate long-term sustainability that benefits all stakeholders.

We believe this requires a rethink about the limits to growth and how publicly listed companies are run as a consequence. It requires a change in mindset. It calls for the governance of companies to become more strategic so that boards have a genuine responsibility for a firm's future and prosperity. And this means the strategy process has to be more collaborative—emerging from the interaction between boards and the CEO.

We came to this subject not as governance experts but from decades of studying and writing about various aspects of strategy and the strategy process. One of the constant themes in our field is to understand why companies fail—with plenty of helpful theories and frameworks having emerged and been implemented over the years to strengthen companies against such failure. But in our own work, we began to recognize that large, listed companies in particular were facing a more systemic challenge that put their long-term survival in peril—in short, the pressure from investors to deliver continual quarterly growth was having a devastating toxic side effect on the strategy process, on investment and resource allocation decisions, and on the culture in many firms.

We saw it firsthand in our research and analysis of the spectacular rise and fall of Nokia in mobile phones. Nokia had been at the forefront of the transformation of the mobile telecommunications industry, which it came to dominate with a global market share of over 40 percent and one of the world's most valuable brands. Yet, within three years, the business dramatically failed, and there was no easy answer as to why. Yes, a succession of poor strategic decisions had been made against a backdrop of stalling underlying growth and investor expectations. And yes, the spirit of collaboration and innovation that had contributed greatly to Nokia's early success had been replaced by infighting, internal competition, and incrementalism as the dominant core business sucked the air from any other initiatives. But there was something missing from this picture.

It may have happened over a shorter time frame, but Nokia's story is not unique. And so we began to ask ourselves, given the tensions between the limited growth in mature businesses and stock market expectations, how can companies escape the growth curse (even though back then we hadn't yet coined that term)? And how can maturity be managed without destroying value and the long-term viability of the firm? We felt these were critical questions because large companies play an important role in wealth creation, knowledge creation, and bringing innovations to market in ways that small companies rarely have the scale or expertise to do (recall the rapid development and rollout of vaccines during the COVID pandemic and the critical role that large pharmaceutical companies played).

Our embryonic thoughts were brought more sharply into focus in 2016, when Andrea Cuomo, a senior executive at STMicroelectronics and long-time collaborator and supporter of our research in the fields of both innovation and alliances, began talking to us about his own observations of companies transitioning from growth to maturity and the crisis this often led to, particularly in fast-moving environments and when the company had the "wrong" shareholders. Over the next few years, we met with Andrea numerous times to discuss this subject, flesh out ideas, and begin to think about high-level "ideal world" solutions to put a stop to the pattern of growth, maturity, and then crisis.

Our work gathered momentum, and the more people we interviewed and the more we read, we realized that at the heart of the problem was a concept of governance, which too often resulted in little more than arm's-length oversight and approval. Boards are, in theory at least, responsible for safeguarding the future of the firm, but it was difficult to see how they could realistically do this without being more engaged in the strategy process. And so, pulling together various threads, we began bridging the hitherto separate worlds of strategy and governance in a bid to propose an alternative to the growth curse.

After our long journey researching and thinking about sustainable corporate longevity, the need to meld the worlds of strategy and governance has become all too apparent to us. However, it's worth noting that, to date, these two important fields have remained resolutely distinct in both theory and practice. In the academic world, strategy scholars rarely venture into governance territory, and vice versa, while in corporate life, the separation is clear, with CEOs and senior executives viewing governance as a regulatory requirement and the board's involvement in strategy being cursory at best. We hope our work will encourage more people to recognize the critical link between the two fields of strategy and governance when it comes to sustainable corporate longevity that benefits the many, not the few, stakeholders.

The fact that this book focuses on publicly listed companies with an Anglo-American-type governance structure is not an oversight or a matter of ignorance; it is a conscious choice we made. Fairly early on in our research, we realized that trying to write this book to cover different types of ownership structure and different models of governance would lead to something unwieldy that would be difficult to follow and extremely long. It seemed to make sense instead to concentrate on the ownership and governance structures that tend to result in the greatest challenges and where the risk of poor strategic decisions is most likely. Having said that, while we have framed the growth curse problem in terms of listed companies with a non-executive board, the solutions we propose to strengthen companies for renewal and prosperity could apply equally well to companies with other ownership and governance structures.

The book is organized into three parts. The first contains the chapters that are concerned with the challenges of the growth curse. Chapter 1 sets the context by looking at the tensions between the urge for growth and the difficulty of finding genuine growth options. While it would be easy to simply put the blame for short-termism on CEOs, chapter 2 examines the pressures that modern CEOs are under, while chapter 3 outlines how those pressures can lead to behaviors that the board should look out for, because they destroy value and ultimately bring about a company's downfall.

Whereas the book's first part explains the magnitude of the problem, the second part is where the manifesto for change begins with a series of chapters relating to the role of the board. Chapter 4 looks at expanding the board's mandate and provides a blueprint for what would constitute a more strategic board. But the ability of a board to perform this more strategic role successfully is dependent on the board being composed of individuals with specific attributes and skills and their ability to work together effectively, all of which are examined in chapter 5. Chapter 6 moves on to the work of the board, specifically by defining the long-term strategy of the company and the tools that can aid in achieving this. In chapter 7, we describe the evolution of strategy failure so that boards can assess the quality of the strategy process in their companies and be aware of, and act on, impending problems before they become full-blown crises. And in chapter 8, we explore how to assess whether the right CEO is in place and the critical factors in selecting a new CEO. We close this chapter by sketching out the working relationship between the board, the CEO, and the executive team.

The final part of the book is where we delve into the specifics of the collaboration between the board and executive in relation to strategic renewal. The importance of the board understanding a company's strategic assets and how they affect both the short- and long-term strategic options open to a firm is the subject of chapter 9. And still focusing on strategic options, chapter 10 investigates how the extent to which a company has strategic sensitivity, leadership unity, and resource fluidity will also determine the strategic paths open to the firm. Together, these two chapters highlight the critical role of strategic governance in guiding a firm toward more sustainable growth and long-term viability. But even the most robust strategic options will only be achievable in a strong and positive culture. Chapter 11 wraps up our examination of strategic renewal by describing how boards can assess the level of energy and commitment in their firms and by outlining suggestions to help revitalize a broken culture.

None of us wants to see companies trapped in the short-termism of the growth curse or see these same companies ultimately fail when the illusion of growth is no longer sustainable. Without doubt, new processes and systems at the executive level and below have a large part to play in ensuring that a company prospers. But we have also come to realize that the most effective way of safeguarding a company's future is through a strategic form of governance in which the board plays a more active role on behalf of all stakeholders, which is what we hope this book will show.

WHEN GROWTH STALLS

There is a great delusion that companies, even large and mature companies, can keep increasing their earnings year-over-year. Most investors expect it, managers buy into it, and governments rely on it. But as is becoming increasingly clear, growth is not eternal. It does stall, and when it does, the past actions of management in creating the illusion of growth are devastating.

This obviously matters to corporate boards, and this book is about what they can do to prevent this situation. But first, in the chapters in Part One, we will take stock of why and how slowing growth leads to damaging leadership actions that ensnare companies in the growth curse.

1 ■ The Growth Conundrum

Crises in corporate governance come in many shapes and sizes. Regardless of whether they are triggered by weak risk management practices, failing strategies, or outright fraud, the root cause of many of these governance troubles is ultimately the same—stalling growth. And as companies mature, this type of slowdown in growth will be a fact of life.

Yet stalling growth seems to be anathema to most CEOs and executive managers. Otherwise, how do you explain why they continue to commit to delivering unrealistic short-term growth—by which we mean bottom-line, net income growth— in the face of what they know to be challenging underlying conditions? Why do corporate leaders in large mature companies seem intent on squeezing every last drop out of their core business in an effort to deliver short-term growth (when these businesses have clearly plateaued) rather than investing in new growth businesses for the longer term? Why is the pretense of continued growth seemingly preferable to issuing a profit warning, especially when missed consecutive quarterly growth forecasts lead management, investors, analysts, the media, and even boards to panic? And why do boards continue to approve strategies designed to favor short-term expediency over longer-term sustainability?

It would be easy to answer these questions by pointing out the obvious: Many influential investors have come to expect (and indeed demand) short-term quarterly growth, and so CEOs and senior executives focus much of their energy on trying to meet this expectation, with the implicit support of their boards. Corporate leaders are afraid of missing quarterly targets; if growth forecasts are lowered or missed, investors don't react well. A company's share price falls on such news, and both the CEO and board are seen to have failed in their fiduciary duty to shareholders. In addition, being pegged to the share price and growth targets, the remuneration of the company's leaders will be adversely affected. So, is it all about loss of esteem and personal financial gain, then? Well, not quite. The growth imperative is highly ingrained in us as humans and cannot be explained away solely by the four Ps—power, prestige, pay, and perks—of a select few.

The pursuit of growth has been vital at both the individual and broader economic levels for human development. It is vital to human inquiry, learning, and creativity. At the individual level, physiological growth aside, humans strive for growth and improvement—whether in education, athletic prowess, artistic and creative skills, wisdom, or spiritually. We grow and improve as parents, in the hobbies and leisure activities we pursue, in the economic security we seek for ourselves and our families, and in our careers. And this career growth imperative is even stronger in many corporate leaders whose success has been based on them continually realizing (and exceeding) their business units' and company's growth objectives.

The orthodoxy of continual and strong corporate growth, which CEOs and senior executives have been imbued with, has in many ways translated into a force for good at the broader economic level, where increased gross domestic product has had an astonishing impact, lifting billions of people out of abject poverty: Since 1950, we have seen the average life expectancy across the world increase by 60 percent to age 72.8.[1] Over the same period, literacy rates increased from just over 50 percent to 87 percent.[2]

But despite the benefits, historically, the pursuit of growth has always had its murkier side—think of colonialism, territorial wars, and the exploitation of natural resources and people on a grand scale. And in recent decades, the relentless commitment to achieving short-term corporate growth based on meeting quarterly targets can be associated with a new set of problems:

A chimera—A focus on short-term quarterly growth rarely delivers sustainable growth but more often the illusion of growth. Leaders can be so fixated on short-termism that meeting quarterly targets becomes sacrosanct at the cost of their own integrity as well as ethical business practice. As we will discuss in detail in chapter 3, delivering the illusion of growth is achieved in a variety of ways, from accounting sleights of hand to outright accounting fraud, as well as by employing handy mechanisms such as share buybacks and waves of acquisitions. Whatever the method, this is not real sustainable growth.

Value destruction—Far from creating value, the scourge of short-termism actually has a detrimental effect on companies in the medium to long term and ultimately hurts shareholders, too (which does not bode well for anyone with investments or a pension fund). A 2017 study by the McKinsey Global Institute of 615 listed companies in the United States, conducted over a 15-year period starting from 2001, found that companies that were managed for the long term (defined as those making consistent investments even in difficult times, whose earnings reflected cash flow not accounting decisions, and those less likely to grow margins to meet short-term targets) outperformed their short-term-oriented peers on many levels. Over the period studied, the revenue of long-term companies was almost 50 percent higher while their net income was, on average, 36 percent higher than the firms with a short-term focus. Additionally, their market capitalization grew more, their shareholder returns were higher, and they created significantly more jobs.[3] This, of course, begs the question: Exactly who benefits from short-termism? Clearly, the executives who enrich themselves while hollowing out the companies they work for benefit. But while the shareholders who put so much pressure on executives to meet quarterly targets gain in the near term, over the relatively short period of 15 years, they are shown to lose out.

Hidden external costs of growth—In general, the external costs of corporate activity (environmental damage, pollution, waste, water and land use, for instance) are not accounted for—although since German sports brand PUMA published the world's first environmental profit and loss in 2011, a small number of companies are beginning to put a financial figure on the environmental costs of their business activities. For companies focused on short-termism, the very idea of stepping up to acknowledge the cost of externalities is anathema, and so the hidden costs of their growth are unlikely to be divulged. In addition, when two common behaviors of short-term-focused companies are taken into account—a lack of investment and "gaming the system"—this points even more strongly to growth being at the cost of the environment and society. Just think back to the Volkswagen emissions scandal and the fact that executives chose to install software that could cheat emissions tests on diesel cars in order to sell more cars, regardless of the damage these engines would have on people's health and the environment more widely.

Despite the ultimate futility of short-termism, the day of reckoning has yet to come. And in the meantime, many boards sit back and allow the circus of conflating corporate progress with increased quarterly results to continue unabated.

The Corporate Growth Trap

Although the world is rapidly changing (and in many respects, such as the calamity of climate change, not for the better), most of today's corporate leaders are products of a time of plenty and opportunity. They belong to an optimistic postwar generation that believes deeply in individualism, progress, and growth.

Financially, the baby-boomer generation has been the most successful ever—some would argue thanks to irresponsibly borrowing from the future and living beyond its means, both financially (national public debt levels have exploded) and environmentally. And though this is the context in which corporate growth has been framed for decades, it's worth reminding ourselves of the major drivers that have supported corporate growth over the years.

The unrelenting pressure for continual and accelerated corporate growth began in earnest in the 1970s with globalization and the "race for the world" as companies sought both scale and arbitrage advantages that only international markets could satisfy. Today, we would argue globalization is a less relevant driver of corporate growth. Advances in flexible and additive manufacturing, which decreases the amount of labor-intensive work needed to make many products, hand-in-hand with wage convergence, is leading to the reshoring of production activities. The beginnings of a similar reshoring of customer service centers is underway, thanks to advances in artificial intelligence and chatbots. Geopolitical and environmental changes are putting global supply chains in jeopardy (think of trade barriers, the Russian invasion of Ukraine, and the increased incidence of flooding resulting from climate change). And we are all only too aware of the COVID pandemic's impact on global trade through lockdowns and restrictions to control the spread of the disease.

The industry convergence we saw take hold almost two decades later in the 1990s added more pressure for rapid growth. To avoid becoming victims of larger firms in converging industries, companies had to become big and strong, either through acquisitions or critical alliances. Although the acceleration of collaboration, alliances, and ecosystems opened new growth opportunities for many companies, partners in these alliances and ecosystems don't reap equal benefits, either in terms of growth or value capture, and so entering into these relationships as a way to spur growth has always been a risky strategy.

Most recently, the emergence of digital platform industries with their natural monopoly characteristics, exploiting increasing returns to adoption[4] and leading to a "winner takes all" outcome, has triggered a fresh round of pressure for rapid growth—helped, of course, by the buzz from social media. With competition becoming more volatile, even companies in the most traditional of industries are pressured to have digital strategies aimed at transforming one-time sales into additional revenues from support and services. But these companies need to tread carefully, because pursuing digital platform growth in a bid to emulate the large internet companies is a fool's errand that delivers little to no real advantage in most industries. But unless regulation and trade barriers curtail the power and dominance of the digital platform companies, digital transformation is likely to continue being a powerful driver of corporate growth across all industries.

It is no wonder, given the many forces that drive the growth imperative (from our natural human instincts to the advantages accrued from aggregate-level economic growth to the changes and trends in the competitive business landscape), that CEOs, senior executives, and managers are addicted to growth, believing that bigger is better. And because of this, leaders find it incredibly difficult to accept and adapt to the reality of slower or stalling growth when their companies reach maturity—or, to put it another way, reach the plateau at the top of an S-curve.

Managing a mature company on the plateau goes against the growth instinct. It calls for a new set of competencies and behaviors that have to be learned. And it requires a board prepared to manage investor expectations while supporting the CEO and executive team in the strategy process to find the next genuine growth opportunities. Without the competencies, processes, and structures to manage a business on the maturity plateau, CEOs and executives become victims of the growth trap. Their very raison d'être is to deliver continuous growth (this is what they are rewarded for, and it is what most investors expect), but no matter how hard they look, major new growth opportunities are very difficult to find.

The Difficulty of Finding New Growth Opportunities
The most obvious response to slowing growth is to look for new growth opportunities that build on a company's existing strengths and capabilities, but this approach is not without risk. New business domains, markets, and ecosystems all require management time, patience, and determination. Take Philips, for instance. Facing a slowdown in many of its mature, legacy business units as a result of severe competition from lower-cost Asian producers, the Dutch firm used its expertise in medical devices as a springboard to transform itself into an integrated healthcare technology firm—divesting its consumer electronics, semiconductor, and lighting businesses in the process.

After initial success (in the first five years after the transformation began, group net income increased around 169 percent), a series of events took their toll on the refocused group, beginning with the recall of sleep apnea machines in 2021, combined with supply chain issues in China and then rising inflation. The board appointed a new CEO who shortly after confirmed the group's commitment to the growth area of integrated healthcare while also announcing that a more nimble and streamlined structure was called for (with a loss of 10,000 jobs by 2025). A transformation of this scale was never going to be easy. But the challenges that Philips has faced in pursuing a major renewal path are undoubtedly less damaging to the long-term survival of the firm than the option of doing nothing when growth was slowing, as this would have eventually brought the company to crisis point.

The list of once-great companies that gradually faded into oblivion is much longer than the list of their peers that have continually prospered by seeking out and developing new growth areas because finding new growth opportunities is very difficult. Although we will explore this in more detail in part III of this book, it is nonetheless worth outlining here a few of the challenges that companies face.

In the example we have just described, Philips was able to pursue a transformation to enter new growth segments because it had a set of strong strategic assets that it was able to leverage in the new businesses it entered; these assets included its capabilities in medical devices, research and development (R&D) and innovation, management systems, and brand. To a large extent, renewal is dependent on transferring existing strategic assets. For companies with weak strategic assets, the search for new growth opportunities becomes much harder and more limited (we discuss the impact of strategic assets on renewal options in detail in chapter 9).

When companies are at their zenith, long before the emergence of any troubling signs that growth might be slowing, finding significant new areas of growth will often fail simply because of the disparity in size between any new growth opportunity and a large core business. Unless they are openly supported by the board and there are very positive signals from the market, CEOs and executive managers will find it difficult to sustain commitment to a relatively small new growth area in the face of a dominant existing business.

Nokia provides a good case in point. As far back as 1995, fearing that the mobile phone market would reach saturation point in the future, Nokia's senior executives began looking for what they called the "third leg" to balance the group's mobile phone and networks businesses. Over the next decade, numerous new venture programs and initiatives all failed to produce that elusive third leg. They were either too far out to be of interest to the business groups or were unable meet the ambitious and unrealistic growth targets imposed by Nokia's leaders.[5] But had Nokia been more sensitive and grounded with its expectations for new venture growth, perhaps it could have found a third leg business.

For companies whose success has been built on a particular technology, no matter how innovative and valuable, over time it becomes increasingly difficult to keep finding new opportunities to leverage this technology. Take W. L. Gore, for example. Since discovering expanded polytetrafluoroethylene in 1969, the company has successfully pioneered its use in a wide range of applications, from waterproof fabrics to medical implants. Yet, according to *Bloomberg BusinessWeek*, this much-lauded company is now vulnerable to the challenges of maturity and needs to find new growth areas[6] at a time when, like its competitors, its core technologies are under ever-greater pressure from increasingly tough environmental regulations.

Another hurdle to finding new growth areas can simply be that they have a very different logic or business model than the core business. For example, going from a single-product business model to complex platforms or ecosystem models can make leaders very reticent about pursuing them. Intel, for example, had long excelled with a simple business model of designing and manufacturing microprocessors that both increased in performance while reducing in cost, which allowed Intel to dominate the market for PCs, laptops, and servers. This model has slowly been running out of steam, though. It has become more difficult, costly, and time-consuming to keep increasing chip performance; at the same time, new demand is shifting to smartphones and gaming consoles.

Although Intel is reacting to these market changes (it has increased R&D spending on gaming chips and made acquisitions to gain a foothold in new areas such as chips for autonomous vehicles), moving from a highly successful monolithic business logic to a wider range of more diversified products across different segments is proving to be quite challenging. A general lack of management skills needed for a more diversified set of businesses is a key barrier; in addition, Intel does not have a good track record for either value-creating acquisitions or renewal efforts.

In some instances, it may not be the difficulty of moving from a simple to a more complicated business model that presents the challenge. Rather, the nature of the business model itself may prevent leaders from seeking out new growth opportunities. Both Kodak and Polaroid famously fell victim to the "razor blade" business models in which the high-margin photographic film they sold brought in such huge profits that any new growth opportunity that could threaten this golden goose was dismissed. And so, despite both companies having developed the necessary technologies to shift to digital photography ahead of many of their global competitors, neither was prepared to cannibalize their highly profitable film-based business model to do so.

But a failure to recognize the potential of a new opportunity, too great a reliance on a single technology, or too divergent a business model are not the only challenges to mature companies finding new growth avenues. Behavior and culture can also play a debilitating role. As successful companies mature, they naturally become strategically myopic (viewing the world through the dominant logic of the core business) and organizationally rigid, meaning their leaders are less likely to see the need for renewal as their time and energy is spent on managing the mature core business. Even if they did, this would call for a massive change in skills and culture away from a focus on operational performance (i.e., running a business efficiently) to creative strategy making (i.e., developing and nurturing new opportunities). And without the processes in place to redeploy resources to foster and monitor new growth opportunities, the core business will continue to dominate internal resource allocation decisions, starving new initiatives of resources. It is clearly easier to focus on what exists than on innovation and renewal.

■

To summarize, the end of growth creates an unprecedented adaptive challenge, with many possible roads to take and no known outcomes. Pursuing new business opportunities is inherently risky, and the payoffs are uncertain and long term. For every success, there will be many that have fallen by the wayside, being too small, too complex, or too late. Perhaps finding new growth opportunities that will move the needle enough to make a significant material difference for a large, mature, and successful company is an illusory hope. What is certain is that given the intense quarterly earnings pressures the leaders of these companies are under, it is not so surprising that few have the time, energy, or inclination to think beyond the short to medium term.

2 ■ The CEO's Mission Impossible

Who Would Want to Be a CEO?

The world isn't short of ambitious and talented managers working their way up the corporate ladder toward a position on the executive team and daring to hope for the ultimate CEO job, provided they have the right skills, connections, timing, and luck. And it's easy to see how the allure of the four Ps—power, prestige, pay, and perks—makes that top spot so coveted.

Yet at the same time, it can be unfathomable why anyone would want to be a CEO today, given the unrealistic growth expectations (maximize short-term shareholder wealth and steer the company toward long-term socially, environmentally, and ethically responsible behavior), incessant pressure, and relentless scrutiny.

Today, CEOs face an ever-increasing and diverse range of external challenges. In little more than the blink of an eye, what once looked like fair-weather sailing can turn into the perfect storm for them and the companies they lead:

Disruption—The risk of becoming a victim of disruption, whether from convergence, substitution, or new business models, is greater than ever, with nimble new challengers emerging quickly and often from unexpected quarters.

Speed—The rate of change is increasing, resulting in pressure for shorter product cycle times and almost real-time responses to changing conditions and demands. This leaves CEOs on the backfoot and constantly firefighting rapidly unfolding situations.

Digital transformation—The pervasive spread of digitalization throughout the value chain has created a double-edged challenge in terms of both developing digital strategies that bring genuine competitive advantage and protecting the company from the vulnerabilities that digitization brings (from technical failures to external hacker attacks).

The unexpected—Unanticipated and unplanned-for events, whether brought about by geopolitical acts such as wars or natural occurrences such as the COVID pandemic or extreme weather, wreak havoc with global supply chains and customer demand, leaving CEOs and their companies exposed and vulnerable.

Regulations—The growing number and frequency of regulatory responses to environmental degradation can impose the phasing out of key legacy technologies and challenge business models in very short time frames.

Ecosystems and alliances—Operating as part of an ecosystem or complex alliance is becoming a fact of life for more companies. Without a thorough understanding of how to manage partnerships, companies can find themselves at the mercy of stronger or more experienced network partners dictating both the strategy of the alliance and the terms of value capture (both of which may not serve all partners equally as well).

Complexity—Increasing complexity makes the job even more difficult as everything CEOs know about how to develop and implement strategy, from forecasting to rigorous planning, no longer holds true. Because the subject of complexity and its impact on management is little understood, we discuss this challenge in more detail later in this chapter.

As companies mature and the growth of the core business slows, these challenges are compounded. CEOs can go from being lauded to being in the crosshairs of shareholders (particularly activists), the media, and potentially the board if a drop in performance contradicts quarterly earnings targets (even if it is just a cyclical blip). So, in a bid to avoid putting themselves in that position, too often CEOs find ways to maintain the illusion of growth, even though it comes at the cost of the long-term sustainability of the companies they lead.

Before looking at the types of destructive behaviors that CEOs adopt to maintain the "illusion of growth" (the subject of chapter 3), it is necessary to understand the context that breeds these practices—namely, the conflicting pressures facing CEOs, the exposure and scrutiny they are under, and a complex environment that they are neither equipped nor able to respond to.

Conflicting Pressures on CEOs

Today, CEOs of listed companies find themselves exposed to a range of conflicting demands from different types of shareholders and stakeholders. But this was not always the case. Back in the 1950s, the organization as an institution had primacy over individual leaders. Charles Erwin Wilson, Benjamin Fairless, and Ralph Cordiner, for example, would not have been household names in 1950 despite running the three biggest companies in the United States at the time: General Motors, US Steel, and General Electric, respectively. During this era, corporations were subject to checks and balances from different stakeholders' groups, including strong government institutions and in many cases powerful unions, but there were few externally driven demands on the governance process. And individuals (as opposed to institutions) made up the largest group of shareholders. This was an era of stakeholder capitalism in which companies tended to be run in the long-term interests of all stakeholders—employees, customers, suppliers, shareholders, and the local communities in which the companies were based.

Things began to change in the 1970s. The first wave of deregulation in industries from aviation to telecommunications and financial services weakened government control mechanisms while a retreat of traditional manufacturing in the United States and Europe cut the strength of unions. Together, these changes effectively gave more power and control to CEOs.

At the same time, the beginnings of an ideological shift from stakeholder to shareholder capitalism was taking root as academic economists used agency theory as a basis of resolving potential conflicts between owners and managers.[1] In essence, they argued that the primary purpose of the firm was to serve the needs of its "owners," and in the case of a publicly listed company, the owners were deemed its shareholders. Thus maximizing shareholder returns should take precedence over the interests of other stakeholders. And to ensure this happened, both controls and management incentives would need to be aligned with this aim.

Over the following two decades, the primacy of shareholder wealth creation became so pervasive that in its statement on corporate governance in September 1997, Business Roundtable (an association representing the CEOs of the leading companies in the United States) said, "The Business Roundtable wishes to emphasize that the principal objective of a business enterprise is to generate economic returns to its owners."[2] (It is worth noting that this statement was not contradicted or challenged until August 2019, when in its statement on the purpose of a corporation, Business Roundtable outlined a "fundamental commitment to *all* of our stakeholders."[3] There has been much debate since about whether the 2019 statement genuinely marked a change in sentiment or was merely a public relations exercise designed to placate the growing chorus of criticism of shareholder capitalism.[4])

Of course, there is a fundamental misunderstanding underlying the primacy of shareholder returns perspective. Contrary to the situation in privately held companies, shareholders of a listed publicly traded company are not legally the owners but residual claimants to its profits.[5]

What is more, speaking of shareholders as if they are an homogeneous group with aligned interests is a fallacy. Different classes of shareholders exhibit very different behaviors driven by very different logics. First, some are speculators, using automated trading and machine learning to hold specific shares for very short time periods—days, hours, or minutes. These traders clearly have little interest in or impact on a company's strategy and do not exert pressure on the CEO or the board.

Next we have the activist hedge fund managers—and here we need to be careful not to tar them all with the same brush. At one extreme, we find the often feared activist hedge fund managers who operate on a similar logic to the old corporate raiders of the 1980s. They target companies in which they see the opportunity for potential gains in the share price from changing the company's strategy, portfolio, or financial structure and buy the minimum level of equity to get a legitimate voice to achieve influence over boards and management, often through costly and distracting proxy battles. Once an activist investor joins the board of a company, the CEO is much more likely to be ousted. Devin Wenig at eBay, Ellen Kullman at DuPont, Myron Ullman at JCPenney, and Emmanuel Faber at Danone are just a few of the many CEOs who have fallen victim to activists.

But even if they don't lose their jobs, activist investors put CEOs and board members under tremendous pressure to deliver short-term financial growth. And activist campaigns are on the rise globally. In 2022, 235 were launched at companies with market capitalization over US$500 million—an increase of 36 percent on the previous year and close to the pre-pandemic high of 249 activist campaigns in 2018.[6]

Although not to such a great extent, another type of activism is also on the rise that puts pressure on CEOs in a different direction. Environment, social, and governance (ESG) funds focus on a range of issues, from environmental sustainability to corruption, and they take companies to task for practices and strategies that fall short in these areas. For example, in 2018, JANA Impact Capital, together with the California State Teachers Retirement System (which at the time held around $2 billion worth of Apple shares), lobbied the tech giant to deal responsibly with the growing issue of children and teenager addiction to devices. Apple responded by introducing screen-time controls.

And it's not just specialist ESG funds that are pressing for greater focus on meeting net-zero targets and more ethical management. Since taking over as CEO of Norway's Norges Bank Investment Management, one of the world's largest sovereign wealth funds, Nicolai Tangen has promised the fund will be active in making proposals on climate initiatives if it deems management and the board are not taking adequate action, and it will vote against what he describes as "corporate greed" in the form of excessive pay.[7]

Then we have the relatively recent rise in the "Big Three" passive index funds—BlackRock, Vanguard, and State Street Global Advisors. According to one study, their combined ownership of Standard and Poor's 500 (S&P 500) companies increased from 7.1 percent in 2000 to 21.9 percent in 2021 (and their proportion of total votes at annual meetings reached 27.5 percent in 2021).[8] The very logic of passive funds makes them de facto long-term investors and their holdings illiquid, but in theory they can still vote against management at annual general meetings and take a stance in proxy contests that send a clear message to management. Their size should also allow them to have a strong voice in conversations with management, and in practice some of their leaders have not shied away from taking positions on issues such as governance, corporate social responsibility, and sustainability. Most notably, in his annual letters to CEOs, Larry Fink, the CEO of BlackRock, regularly urges the leaders of companies in which BlackRock holds shares toward a more responsible form of capitalism.[9]

However, research on the Big Three index funds has found passivity to be a defining trait in how they engage with the companies in their portfolios, and so their impact on the management of these companies is questionable. Their investment in stewardship is negligible (estimated at around 0.2 percent of the fees they charge), and in the period from 2017 to 2019, the Big Three had no engagement at all with 92.5 percent of the companies in their portfolios. What's more, between 2007 and 2018, the Big Three did not make any nominations to select directors to the boards of companies in their portfolios.[10] This obviously has implications for governance particularly if the Big Three continue to expand their ownership in large companies over the coming years.

The aim of another class of shareholder, active investors, particularly the large funds, is to beat the market by leveraging their in-house analysts to identify potential strategic problems at companies in their portfolios before they become widely known and then use this information to create trading gains for themselves. So it is not in their interest to share their analysis with management or the board because by doing so, they would lose their competitive advantage.

Many different types of investors look to the reports of equity analysts as guidance about the effectiveness of management, company strategies, and their relative strength and weaknesses across various time horizons. This puts equity analysts in a very powerful position and drives CEOs to short-term behavior to meet analysts' quarterly expectations, because failing to do so can cause investors to sell and the share price to drop. It has been shown that the more analysts cover a particular company, the lower the likelihood of that company making long-term capital investments because management is under such intense pressure to deliver short-term results.[11]

Harking back to our earlier discussion of the growth imperative, the long period of sustained economic growth in the United States since the 2008 recession led to yet another source of growing pressure on CEOs. Investors and managers alike have wholeheartedly bought into the notion that high-income growth can be sustained forever. Yet the statistics behind this thinking are misleading, as the extraordinary rise of a handful of tech firms—Google (now Alphabet), Facebook (now Meta), and Apple—accounts for a disproportionate share of this growth. In addition, prior to 2022, the era of ultra-low interest rates allowed companies to become more highly leveraged and resulted in debt at nonfinancial sector corporates accounting for almost half of gross domestic product in the United States by 2019.[12] With interest rates and inflation on the rise, paying down this debt will be even more difficult if profits slow (as they did as a result of the COVID pandemic) and will leave corporate leaders more vulnerable than ever.

At the same time, CEOs are now countering a new societal force, unleashed by millennials and Generation Z, many of whom believe that doing good is more important than doing well and wish to see companies behave in environmentally and socially responsible ways. And being a social-media-savvy generation, they are quick to let their displeasure at corporate behavior be known. For instance, in October 2019, in an embarrassing incident for oil giant BP, the Royal Shakespeare Company was forced to end BP's sponsorship following a campaign by young people who were unhappy that the arts organization took money from a company that they believed was destroying their futures. Over the coming years, the largest transfer of wealth ever will take place with the passing of the baby-boomer generation. And with the millennials and Generation Z as the new holders of company equity, they will find themselves in a much more powerful position to demand that companies do good.

CEOs Are More Exposed than Ever

As these various forces pull them in different directions, CEOs also find themselves and their actions open to greater scrutiny than ever before.

In tandem with the transition from stakeholder to shareholder capitalism, we saw the rise of the celebrity CEO and a time in which success was gauged not only by how rapidly you grew your company but how often you graced the covers of *Fortune, Newsweek,* or *Time* magazines. As distinct from founder CEOs, who have always held the public's imagination (think of Walt Disney, Henry Ford, and Thomas Edison to Bill Gates, Richard Branson, and Steve Jobs), a new wave of professional manager CEO began to step into the limelight. The first of these was probably Lee Iacocca, the president of Ford and then CEO of Chrysler, who appeared in advertisements for company products and on magazine covers and even wrote a best-selling autobiography.

Gradually, the pervasiveness of the celebrity CEO resulted in the personalization of corporate success or failure in the business press—the fate of huge, diversified, complex global companies was deemed to be down to one man (or, more rarely, one woman). Jack Welch is one of the most obvious exemplars of this trend. Welch gained iconic status during his 20-year tenure at the helm of GE, overseeing a staggering 2,829 percent increase in the market capitalization of the firm and making it the most valuable company in the world by the time he retired in 2001. In addition to his ruthless pursuit of growth, Welch was also famed for creating the GE management style—which many other companies sought to emulate. He courted the media, was a much-sought-after conference speaker, taught at business schools, and even loaned his name to a management institute and GE's global research and technology center. However, as GE's troubles have become increasingly apparent in more recent years, the reputation of Welch has been tarnished, and just as he was once lionized for GE's success, he is now being vilified for its failure.

This glorification of successful CEOs led to the growing pay gap between CEOs and their employees. The true extent of this became apparent in 2018, when under the Dodd–Frank Act, listed companies had to disclose pay ratios for the first time, and it was revealed that the compensation of the average CEO of an S&P 500 company was 287 times greater than that of their median employees. By comparison, the Economic Policy Institute estimated that in 1978, this difference was only 30 times more. Between 1978 and 2018, when adjusted for inflation and based on realized stock options, CEOs saw their compensation increase by 940 percent, significantly more than the 11.9 percent wage growth that average employees saw and also at least 25 percent more than stock market growth over the same period.[13]

These levels of high pay have exposed CEOs even further. No CEO is perfect, but their remuneration would imply otherwise, and soaring compensation packages have attracted increasingly critical attention in the press. In 2022, the total compensation of Peter Kern of Expedia ($296 million), Coty Inc.'s Sue Nabi ($283 million), David Zaslav of Warner Bros. Discovery ($246 million), Andrew Jassy of Amazon ($212 million), and Intel's Patrick Gelsinger ($178 million),[14] among others, came in for particular ire from the media.

As in so many things, where the United States leads, others follow, and so it is with the trend of excessive CEO pay at listed firms elsewhere in the world (though the levels of pay tend to be slightly less excessive). In 2022, in the United Kingdom, the highest-paid CEO at a Financial Times Stock Exchange (FTSE) listed company was Sebastien De Montessus of Endeavour Mining (£16.85 million).[15] In France, Carlos Tavares, CEO of Stellantis, topped the earnings list (€66 million).[16] Stephen Angel, head of Dax-listed Linde, was Germany's highest earner (€14 million).[17] In Japan, the director of Z Holdings Corp., Jungho Shin, headed the list of public company earners (¥4.335 billion—approximately $32 million).[18] The highest-paid CEO of a listed company in India was HCL's C Vijayakumar (INR 131 crore—approximately $16.5 million).[19] While in Australia, Macquarie Group's Shemara Wikramanayake was the top earner for the second consecutive year (AU$23.7 million—approximately $16 million).[20]

Paradoxically, correlation studies have shown that higher CEO compensation is not associated with higher performance; in fact, the opposite is true—higher pay appears to be linked with lower performance.[21] We all know correlation is not causation, but the casual insight goes like this: Highly paid CEOs become overconfident. They are more willing to take higher risks—for example, to overinvest or undertake difficult mergers and acquisitions—and they are also more likely to engage in empire building. Even if the logic of these deals does not make sense in the cold light of day, their pride and hubris in believing they will succeed drive them forward into actions that undercut future performance. And boards are too often in thrall to the high-profile CEO they hired to question or oppose these types of value-destroying strategies.

Eye-wateringly high golden parachute settlements and guaranteed retirement benefits, which are paid regardless of performance, also provoke public and media incredulity. After failing to turn around Yahoo, Marissa Mayer left the firm with $23 million in severance payments. Having run Royal Bank of Scotland into the ground so that it needed a £45 billion UK taxpayer bailout, CEO Fred Goodwin walked away with a £700,000 per year pension (though he subsequently agreed to reduce this amount by half). Leo Apotheker was fired by HP after only 11 months in the CEO role; nonetheless, he received a $9.6 million severance package. And Timothy Leuliette, CEO of Visteon from 2012 until 2015, won a $16.7 million golden parachute settlement, despite being pushed out in a pornography and prostitution scandal.

It is not just in the media that CEOs are now more visible than ever. The unrelenting short-term earnings pressures imposed by equity analysts and certain shareholders put CEOs under constant scrutiny to meet quarterly performance indicators. As humans, we have very high rates of discount when it comes to allocating our attention—events on the near-term horizon garner much more attention than those with longer lead times. Given this, it is not surprising that for many CEOs, meeting short-term targets takes precedence over the quality of the long-term strategy. The pressure and the payoffs are more immediate, and few CEOs survive missing more than a handful of quarterly earnings forecasts.

Particularly when activist shareholders are circling and the press are speculating, instead of protecting or buffering the CEO from investor disquiet, their own sense of panic can mean boards themselves become a source of pressure for the CEO. Having been groomed for the position for years, Mark Fields became CEO of Ford in 2014 and led the company to its highest earnings in its history. At the same time, to position Ford for the future technological shift the industry was facing, he invested a significant portion of the company's profits into research and development (R&D). Ford's share price tumbled, and the board came under increasing pressure from shareholders to focus on boosting the share price. They finally acquiesced, firing Fields in 2017. Another successful CEO who fell victim to a combination of shareholder pressure and board panic was Ellen Kullman at DuPont. Under Kullman's leadership, DuPont was outperforming the S&P 500 as well as positioning itself for the future by refocusing on core R&D. Then, in 2015, after a narrowly won proxy battle against activist investor Nelson Peltz, a strong dollar coupled with lower Chinese demand resulted in reduced earnings. DuPont's board was unnerved, and Ellen Kullman abruptly announced her retirement.

The Challenges of Greater Complexity

Not only are CEOs and their leadership teams subject to increasingly intense contradictory pressures to increase short-term profits, protect the long-term viability of their companies, and behave in an environmentally and socially ethical way, but they are expected to do this in the context of a much more complex world.

Complexity is profoundly disturbing for corporate leaders. Over their careers, they have honed their skills in a world in which their mastery of linear models, rigorous planning, accurate forecasting, and disciplined judgment gave rise to their personal success. Complexity, though, takes CEOs and senior executives out of their comfort zones and leaves them facing a new set of hurdles that radically challenge their mental models, their sense of self, their behavior as leaders, and the structures within which they operate.[22] (Figure 2.1 outlines the impediments that leaders face in complex contexts.)

Complexity presents CEOs and senior managers with significant cognitive hurdles. The pressure and rewards for delivering measurable quarterly results lead to a short-term bias that

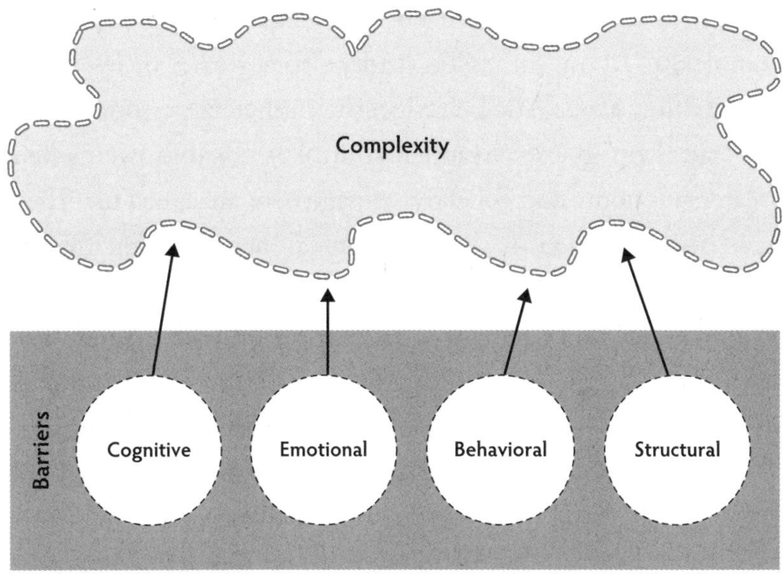

Figure 2.1: Managing in Complex Environments

makes leaders so preoccupied with immediate issues that they fail to see the "weak signals" of emerging problems. Furthermore, throughout their careers, managers learn the importance of presenting "logical narratives" both inside the firm and externally to investors, partners, customers, and the media. These overly rational explanations fail to take account of the fact that the world is complex and messy and, in doing so, overlook the likelihood of low-probability, high-impact events (or black swan events, as Nassim Nicholas Taleb termed them).[23] This tendency toward the simple and logical is underpinned by a cognitive focus on structured data (which is in fact better at illuminating the past than shining a light on the future). Many management decisions are based on extrapolation from retrospective management accounting data. Although this seems to provide an assurance of certainty against which decisions can be argued, cognitively, it limits the absorptive capacity of managers to recognize and integrate conflicting and fuzzy data.

Emotionally, leaders are no better equipped to deal with complexity. Many successful leaders (to a greater or lesser extent) exhibit narcissistic behavior; their inherent personal agendas lead them to exert as much control as possible, even when greater autonomy and collective engagement are called for. They have been schooled in the tradition of "heroic leadership" in which a strong CEO has all the answers (and few would dare to admit they don't). A fear of failure (mixed with a good dose of egotism) drives the need to appear to be successful and also a reluctance to gamble a known present for an uncertain future.

Closely related to the cognitive and emotional barriers are a range of behavioral impediments that challenge leaders in complex environments. The "planning instinct" is ingrained in most leaders based on assumed linear cause-and-effect relationships, so they do not appreciate the systemic nature of complexity. Faced with a problem, they modularize it and ignore interdependencies. And they will only act when the odds of success can be assessed. "Technical leadership" encourages problem solving using familiar tools and processes and industrial-age mental models. And here, the influence of consultants comes into play as leaders prefer to rely on the inputs of these known advisers over a wider range of diverse sources. Too often, CEOs behave as the strong leader favoring decisive decision-making over the collaborative exploration of emergent ideas while engaging in debate (rather than dialogue) to reach the "right" answer. They see leadership as a position, not an act.

Finally, structural barriers in organizations are a challenge to leaders in complex environments. Hierarchical bureaucracies impose a clear division of labor and separate expertise into silos, rendering the cross-fertilization of ideas and knowledge sharing all but impossible. Their processes are designed to deliver efficiency and to optimize routine operations in stable conditions, not to cope with emergence and complexity. Effectiveness is often sacrificed at the altar of efficiency as rigid structures leave little to no flexibility to adapt to change.

Even without the barriers outlined above that leaders face today, complex environments make it impossible to forecast with any degree of accuracy how events might unfold, rendering tried-and-tested strategic decision-making guidelines and processes much less effective than they once were. Strategy implementation becomes equally difficult, as the outcomes of one's actions are impossible to assess because of unanticipated second- and third-order consequences and the emergent feedback loops they drive. Although great strides have been made in modeling "organized" complexity[24]—for example, the movement of crowds and flocks of birds whose members follow simple rules—unfortunately, no such progress has been made with understanding the type of "disorganized" complexity.[25] This is the complexity facing corporate leaders today, in which there are a large number of variables with unpredictable behavior. This leaves CEOs and senior managers in yet another impossible predicament because they are expected (and financially incentivized) to deliver predictable quarterly growth, yet most of them simply do not have the tools, processes, capabilities, or behaviors necessary to do so in a complex world.

Complexity calls for strategic reactiveness to seize unexpected opportunities and fight unanticipated threats in a fast and agile way. And so the much vaunted ability to create, communicate, and commit to a "vision," attributed to CEOs from Nokia's Jorma Ollila to IBM's Lou Gerstner, is of little use when up against the uncertainty brought about by complexity. Pursuing a vision implies charting a course toward a long-term goal, but in a complex world, flexibility and adaptability trump adherence to a vision. Instead, a clear sense of purpose combined with wisdom and virtue[26] should guide decision-making so that leaders are able to make the right choices given the available information and aligned with the company's values.

As traditional management tools along with their own leadership capabilities become less effective, we would argue that the much-used VUCA acronym (volatility, uncertainty, complexity, and ambiguity) takes on a more ominous meaning for CEOs. They feel vulnerable, unaware/uninformed, confused, and anxious. And like many people in power, and with much to lose, corporate leaders fear the unknown.

3 ■ The CEO's Wrong Response?

The sense of fear and VUCA feelings (vulnerable, unaware/uninformed, confused, and anxious) that many CEOs now experience should not be surprising given the significant and often contradictory pressures they are under, the greater exposure they face, and the increasing complexity of the world in which they operate. And their situation only gets worse as a company matures, growth slows or reaches a plateau, and the crucial alignment between a company's leadership, board members, and investors comes under increasing strain. The tension between the continual short-term growth a CEO is expected to deliver and the reality of a company's operating environment can tempt leaders to "misbehave" in order to give the illusion of growth—the impression of good short-term performance, even if this comes at the cost of compromising the longer-term future of the company.

As we shall see, this misbehavior can fall anywhere on a spectrum from the short-sighted to the ethically questionable to the outright fraudulent. While the adoption of these types of behavior will always be known to a greater or lesser extent within the management ranks, it is rare for executives or managers to put themselves at personal risk by becoming whistleblowers. So who should be monitoring the CEO and senior executives for signs of wrongdoing? And who should be looking out for the telltale signs that all is not as well as it might at first sight seem? Naturally, it is the duty of the board to protect the company, its investors, and all stakeholders. In the following pages, we outline the common misbehaviors that should set alarm bells ringing and that a board should look out for.

Causes and Justifications

For the most part, CEOs and their managers who engage in deceit to game the system in order to meet market expectations are not bad or malevolent people. Nor is the misconduct they perpetrate the rare exception we might hope. A study of Fortune 100 companies found that over a five-year period, 40 percent of leaders were caught up in wrongdoing allegations that were serious enough to be covered in the media.[1] It would seem that under pressure to keep investors happy, keep the board happy, meet performance pay targets, and keep their professional reputations intact, CEOs and their senior teams may overlook their moral compass and misrepresent the truth to overcome "bumps" in performance, especially if given the opportunity by a lack of effective monitoring and controls. If their deception is not caught and also results in positive rewards, their wrongdoing will likely escalate—particularly if the underlying performance problem has not been addressed and is getting worse.

The deception will also grow in terms of the number of people involved and become an organization-level phenomenon as pressure mounts on managers throughout the company to "meet their numbers" or risk losing their jobs.[2] Those in power should never underestimate the fear they can instill in their staff of bringing bad news to light. When Alan Mulally arrived as CEO of the troubled Ford Motor Company, he found a culture of burying bad news in favor of relentlessly optimistic (and unrealistic) forecasts, which he noticed differed depending on the target audience. Managers throughout the company were so afraid of revealing bad news that it took Mulally months to convince them that transparency was the only way they could turn the company around.

As both the scope and scale of misrepresentation grow within an organization, CEOs and executives assuage their guilt by rationalizing their behavior using "techniques of neutralization" (originally described in 1957 by American sociologists Gresham Sykes and David Matza to explain the behavior of deviant teenagers).[3] They justify their wrongdoing by convincing themselves they had no choice, no one was harmed, and in fact the outcome of their behavior is actually beneficial.

Most CEO misbehavior does not violate the letter of the law, even if it pushes the boundaries of the spirit of the law. The number of leaders, like Enron's Jeff Skilling and WorldCom's Bernie Ebbers, who have crossed the line and committed criminal acts in order to sustain the appearance of growth is thankfully small. But even the best-intentioned CEOs can fall into the trap of creating a culture in which "meeting the numbers" becomes the raison d'être of management, and as we have seen with many once-mighty companies, this never ends well.

GE is a case in point. From the time when Jack Welch became CEO (1981), a culture was built around delivering numbers to keep Wall Street happy, with earnings per share (EPS) becoming one of the most critical metrics for GE businesses. In addition, research that had begun at GE in the 1960s suggested a strong correlation between market share and profitability. This was interpreted as causality by GE senior managers, leading to an internal rule being imposed that every business had to be either first or second in its sector to remain in the GE family. This meant managers became adept at defining the market so narrowly they could claim to be number one or two. They also focused on cutting costs, headcount, and product lines, while the drumbeat of market share meant salespeople were incentivized on volume not margins. After decades of continually beating earnings estimates, a strong sense of optimism and confidence had developed in GE. But that confidence was built on sand. GE had employed the gambit of misbehaviors to give the illusion of growth.

Share Buybacks

Thanks to weak and largely unenforceable regulation (in the United States at least), share buybacks can be a very convenient tool for manipulating quarterly performance targets because they inflate EPS and increase a company's share price while potentially providing the added bonus of huge payouts for executives. And share buybacks are on the rise: S&P 500 firms spent a record $881.7 billion on buybacks in 2021, up almost 70 percent from 2020 and over 9 percent higher than the pre-pandemic high of 2018.[4] While in the United Kingdom, FTSE

100 companies recorded the highest level of buybacks ever in 2022.[5] That same year across Europe's 11 largest markets, the value of buybacks doubled year-over-year.[6]

There is a line of argument that these figures do not reveal the full and accurate picture of how much cash companies are returning to shareholders. To do this, one would need to look at the net figure of buybacks and dividends minus both direct and indirect (i.e., staff compensation) equity issuances (and in the nine years to 2016, US-listed firms issued shares of around $2.3 trillion in compensation alone).[7] On this basis, then, companies are not returning nearly as much cash to shareholders as it would initially appear. In defense of buybacks, one could also make an argument, following a Schumpeterian logic, that returning cash to shareholders provides a mechanism for those investors to then channel their resources away from mature companies with low short-term growth potential toward more innovative high-growth firms.

And as long as a company has excess cash after investments, a strong balance sheet, and free cash flow (so future growth is not at risk), and provided the company also times its buybacks when its shares are not overpriced, then buying back shares seems a logical route to return cash to shareholders. Unfortunately, when CEOs are either scrambling to meet earnings targets or planning to enrich themselves, these conditions are rarely met. The result is both value-destroying for shareholders and dangerous for the long-term viability of the company. For example, in 2008, instead of investing in the troubled company's future, Antonio Perez, CEO of Kodak, launched a $1 billion share buyback program paying an average price per share of $15.01. By year end, the share price was under $7, and three years later, Kodak filed for Chapter 11 bankruptcy.

GE's leaders had similarly engaged in ill-advised share buy-backs instead of investing in the fundamentals of the company, in what has been described in *Fortune* magazine as wasting billions of dollars buying shares at inflated prices in "one of the most value-destroying repurchase programs in the annals of corporate America."[8] For a long time that we now know the company was actually struggling, the buyback strategy seemed to be working for GE's leaders—from 2008 to 2015, GE spent $27.8 billion repurchasing shares and hit its EPS targets in all but one quarter during that period. In the 10 years up to the end of 2017, GE spent almost $54 billion buying back shares at an average of $26 per share. By the close of trading at the end of 2018, GE's share price was $7.28, and the company had little cash left to undertake the restructuring it needed.

Obfuscating Waves of Distracting Acquisitions

Another area in which GE's leaders delivered short-term growth while destroying value was the merry-go-round of acquisitions and divestments for which the company had to write down $23 billion in 2018. Under CEOs Jack Welch and Jeff Immelt, the drive for market leadership had seen GE's business groups constantly buying and selling companies—and this was made easier thanks to having a de facto in-house bank, GE Capital. But much of this activity was hiding a relatively lackluster performance in GE's industrial units. And worse still, GE had overpaid for many of the companies it bought. In the case of its 2015 acquisition of the poorly performing French manufacturer of power turbines, Alstom, GE's timing was also rather disastrous. Although the $10.6 billion acquisition propelled GE's power division to being the world's largest producer of gas turbines, it came at a time that growth in renewables meant global demand for fossil fuel–based power generation equipment was crashing. Taken together with huge liabilities from Alstom's sales contracts, three years later, GE announced it would be writing down the entire purchase price of Alstom.

According to *The Economist*, in 2017, GE's acquisitions and divestments had increased to the equivalent of 167 percent of its capital employed while its returns had barely moved. Clearly, GE had overpaid for many of its acquisitions, and when considering both the costs of integration and weak operating performance, the group's cash flows resembled 2001 levels.[9] So, despite a frenzy of merger and acquisition (M&A) activity increasing capital and giving the appearance of growth, GE had in fact destroyed value by failing to deliver a commensurate growth in earnings from its increased asset base.

It can be difficult for boards to assess the strategic value of the acquisition proposals brought to them. While some proposals will definitely fall into the category of the obfuscating, there are genuine and legitimate reasons to acquire companies (despite integration difficulties and uncertainty about whether the investment will create or destroy value). In consolidating industries, for instance, acquisitions can be the most timely route to ensure a company's survival, as we have seen in a range of industries, from pharmaceuticals to banking. In the fast-moving consumer goods sector, buying smaller innovative companies can be the most efficient and least risky way of keeping in line with changing consumer preferences—consider, for example, Unilever's 2019 acquisitions of skin care companies Tatcha and Garancia and its 2017 purchase of organic herbal tea producer Pukka. In industries undergoing disruption, companies can find themselves in a race to acquire new opportunities such as in fintech or environmentally friendly technologies for heating, insulation, or power generation. And finally, acquisitions can provide access to specific technologies and knowledge needed for continual innovation. Instrument maker Yamaha, for example, acquired French loudspeaker business XEXO and US provider of wireless audio solutions Revolabs to support innovation in its world-leading digital keyboards.

However, given that most estimates put the failure rate of M&A activity of actually creating value at somewhere between 70 and 90 percent, it follows that analyzing any proposed acquisition always involves an act of faith that the acquired entity will be successfully integrated and the proverbial synergies will prove real rather than elusive. Even so, acquisitions will usually bolster the bottom line for a few years, and for CEOs and executive teams who engage in continual streams of acquisitions, by the time it becomes clear an acquisition has destroyed value, it will likely escape scrutiny because attention will be focused on the company's more recent acquisitions and the excitement around the latest targets. According to our colleague Annet Aris, a seasoned nonexecutive director, executives get away with this because most acquisitions have to be approved by the board in a rush. She added, "Often CEOs try and keep acquisitions low profile, casting them as incremental decisions, each small enough not to draw in-depth attention from the board. What they do may be legal, but it's still an unethical misrepresentation."[10]

Clearly, GE isn't alone in employing an M&A sleight of hand—it would seem to be common practice that rarely ends well. During Percy Barnevik's eight-year tenure as CEO at multinational engineering firm ABB, he oversaw the acquisition of 240 companies. In its haste to acquire, ABB did not always conduct thorough due diligence, and this failure (together with general poor group performance) brought the company to the brink of bankruptcy in 2001 as asbestos liabilities in the United States from the 1989 acquisition of Combustion Engineering cost ABB over $2 billion. HP is another company whose rush to acquire has not always paid off. Its controversial merger with Compaq Computer was aimed at entering a low-margin segment that was already in decline. In 2008, HP paid almost $14 billion for Electronic Data Systems (EDS), but only four years later wrote down $8 billion on the acquisition; in 2010, in a bid to enter the mobile market, HP acquired Palm for $1.2 billion, invested an additional $2.1 billion in the firm, only to write down the entire $3.3 billion investment at the end of 2011. That same year, despite a lack of strategic fit, HP paid $11.1 billion for software company Autonomy, only to write down $8.8 billion of the value of Autonomy the following year. It is clear CEOs and executive teams can use acquisitions, big or small, to divert attention away from a company's slowing growth and its lack of a viable long-term strategy.

Misleading, Borderline, or Fraudulent Accounting

While these diversions can be effective up to a point, companies can also employ a range of accounting tricks to conceal bad news by giving the appearance that performance targets have been met, when in reality the business is stagnating or shrinking. And once again, GE provides a salutary lesson in the use of "earnings management" and selective disclosures to manipulate financial results. It was only in April 2017, when GE announced a cash flow shortfall of $1 billion, that investors and the outside world finally realized the extent of problems in some of GE's businesses, which for years had been hidden behind aggressive and creative accounting practices designed to deliver revenue and profit targets.

It came to light, for example, that GE Power had prematurely booked sales of almost $100 million just before quarter's end in order to meet targets.[11] And when it came to manipulation, GE executives found another rich seam to mine in the group's huge portfolio of contract assets (service contracts to maintain equipment and systems supplied by GE's Power and Aviation businesses, usually lasting for between 10 and 30 years). Many contracts were renegotiated to give customers discounts in exchange for paying earlier—even though this decreased the value of the contract over the long term. And when possible, the terms of contracts were adjusted—for instance, to provide more upgrades to increase their profitability. According to a report in the *Wall Street Journal*, "In the first nine months of 2017, earnings stemming from the increase in contract assets amounted to $1.93 billion, . . . more than half the company's pretax earnings from continuing operations."[12] But GE's accounting manipulations didn't end there. In order to boost short-term cash flow, the power division had also sold its receivables to GE Capital. In fact, GE Capital had provided a handy vehicle for trading assets and liabilities with the group's industrial businesses to help them meet their quarterly earnings.

What is arguably most surprising about GE's accounting practices is that they continued as long as they did, given that in 2009, GE had been investigated by the Securities and Exchange Commission (SEC) for alleged improper accounting methods to increase reported earnings and avoid reporting negative financial results. On completing the investigation, Robert Khuzami, director of the SEC's Enforcement Division, stated, "GE bent the accounting rules beyond the breaking point," while his colleague David Bergers added, "Every accounting decision at a company should be driven by a desire to get it right, not to achieve a particular business objective. GE misapplied the accounting rules to cast its financial results in a better light."[13] Settling the case cost GE $50 million. Yet, despite this investigation and public censure, 10 years later, GE found itself once again being investigated by the SEC for accounting irregularities relating to the service contracts.

Perhaps somewhat naively, we would assume annual external audits should deter executives from fiddling the accounts and, failing that, protect shareholders and stakeholders from any misleading accounting practices. Yet too often, auditors fail to pick up on accounting errors, and this calls into question whether they are complicit or merely incompetent. The auditing arm of Arthur Andersen signed off on the accounts of Enron (which was hiding debt in off-balance sheet entities) and WorldCom (which had not only made an undisclosed $400 million loan to its founder CEO but had $14 billion worth of accounting errors) just before the bankruptcy of both companies. These colossal scandals did bring down the accounting side of Arthur Andersen but obviously failed to send a big enough shockwave to encourage higher standards in the industry. For eight years, PwC auditors failed to notice a $600 million fraud committed by Tyco's chief executive and chief financial officers. For decades, KMPG has given GE's accounts a clean bill of health, despite the firm's web of accounting irregularities. Meanwhile, in the United Kingdom, EY (formerly Ernst and Young) is under investigation by the Financial Reporting Council for signing off on the accounts of Thomas

Cook, the world's oldest travel company, just before the firm went into bankruptcy, and Deloitte received a record £15 million fine for failings in its auditing of software firm Autonomy.

Speeding Up Decline

By engaging in the wrong responses to slowing growth and instead shoring up the illusion of growth, CEOs are unwittingly falling victim to the growth curse, speeding up decline and putting the long-term future of their companies in jeopardy. Under pressure and caught in a vortex of contradictory demands, they can lose perspective. Instead of focusing on the difficult and complex arena of strategy making, they instead retreat into the much simpler world of operational efficiency, where quick wins are not only much easier to come by but will have a more immediate, positive impact on those all-important performance ratios. An operationally focused CEO who is always managing to the bottom line is much more likely to cut vital long-term strategic resource commitments.

Having been an innovation powerhouse, where risk-taking, tolerance of failure, and a long-term outlook were imbued in the culture, 3M suffered when it hired an operationally focused CEO, James McNerney. During his time at 3M, the share price almost doubled. However, it came at a cost, and by 2005, when Sir George Buckley took over as CEO, despite good quarterly results, the company was losing market share, and its percentage of sales from products introduced in the previous five years was at its lowest ever, as was customer satisfaction. In a candid interview in the *Financial Times* some years later, Sir George explained, "This was a company on a glide path to disaster yet the external indicators at the surface level all looked fine. But it was a company that was sick. If we had not reversed course, this company would have become another Kodak, I'm absolutely convinced about that."[14] To set 3M back on a path of long-term sustainability, Sir George refocused the company on continual innovation and abandoned quarterly financial reporting.

In listed companies, it takes a very self-assured and courageous CEO to eschew the tyranny of short-term quarterly earnings in favor of long-term prosperity. And for the majority of CEOs and senior executives whose careers have been based solely in the world of shareholder capitalism (and have greatly prospered from it), they more than likely lack the skills as well as the mindset to change.

So this begs some questions: If neither the CEO nor investors have the incentives and skills, who can step forward to worry about the long-term strategy of companies as more than just a succession of tomorrows? Who should be responsible for steering companies away from the environmental damage and societal inequalities overlooked by the shareholder capitalism growth model toward a fairer and more sustainable stakeholder model? Who will be able to shield the CEO from undue investor pressures and work with them to protect the firm for now and the future? Who will be able to mobilize the resources in an increasingly complex environment to anticipate the future and the opportunities it may offer? And who will have the power and authority to take action?

PART TWO

A NEW DEAL AT THE TOP

Why Strategy Matters for Governance

Boards have become part of the problem. In adopting a passive monitoring role, board mandates have at best limited their involvement and understanding, and at worst, many have been asleep on the job, unaware of the troubles brewing in the companies they oversee (think of the cases of GE and Boeing). Part Two explores how boards can become part of the solution to ensuring the long-term viability of the company, allowing it to overcome the growth curse.

4 ■ Broadening the Board's Mandate

We have seen how easy it is for CEOs and senior managers to be tempted by short-term expediency. A confluence of factors, including the relentless pressure from certain shareholder groups for steady and continuous quarterly growth, the way CEO compensation packages are structured, and the practical challenges of effective strategy making in an increasingly complex environment, can make it difficult for them to make the right choices for the long-term viability of a firm and all its stakeholders. And this becomes even more of a challenge when a firm is facing maturity. At a time when the rate of growth naturally slows, senior management becomes so focused on milking legacy technologies, systems, processes, and assets for marginal growth gains that they fail to focus on or invest in future opportunities—they fall victim to the growth curse.

So, if the executive management team are ill equipped to guard against the vagaries of short-termism and protect the long-term future of a firm by themselves, who is best positioned to take the reins and navigate a mature firm toward purpose and progress? Should the board step into the breach and more actively guide management toward longer-term strategic considerations? And if, as we believe, they are uniquely in a position to do this, in what ways will boards have to change how they operate to take on a more collaborative strategic role? But first, let us look at potential impediments to more strategically active boards.

Boards Are Also Under Increasing Pressure

The CEO and executive management team are not alone in finding their roles becoming increasingly difficult. Boards of directors are also facing contradictory pressures and under greater exposure to public scrutiny than ever before. On the one hand, they face pressure from certain types of investors and potentially their own management teams to support strategies that will deliver strong quarterly earnings first and foremost. And yet, on the other hand, they are responsible for safeguarding the future of the firm for all stakeholders. They may find themselves being legally responsible for two things that can be diametrically opposed, and in a mature firm, putting the short-term financial interests of "owners" first is not only failing the long-term viability of the firm but potentially hastening its demise.

Direct Shareholder Pressures

As we discussed in chapter 2, shareholders are understandably motivated by their own self-interest and time horizons. It would be illusory to expect otherwise. Too often, though, the interests and limited time horizons of a minority of very vocal shareholders may not be in the best interests of the long-term prosperity of the firm.

In recent decades with the rise in both concerns for shareholder wealth and worries about risks of misalignment between shareholders' interests and management actions, the main responsibility of the board has largely been seen as one of ex-post oversight and monitoring to protect the interests of shareholders against possible mismanagement by the CEO. The primacy of agency theory in conceptualizing the relationship between the board and management has accentuated its potentially adversarial nature when, in fact, the board should be perfectly positioned to actively protect executives from investor pressures by guiding shareholders to modify their expectations and encouraging them to be more patient.

Yet shareholder pressure on boards does not just come in the form of the desire to protect returns on investment. The rise in shareholder lawsuits being brought against individual directors of listed firms since the financial crisis indicates that certain groups of shareholders are increasingly focused on the ethical and safety standards of the companies they invest in.[1] In March 2019, a lawsuit brought by shareholders against the directors of Wells Fargo, claiming they had failed in their fiduciary duty when millions of fake accounts were opened, was settled for US$240 million. Meanwhile, 12 directors of Google's parent company, Alphabet, faced a shareholder lawsuit for allegedly covering up sexual harassment claims against senior executives (which was settled in 2020). And Alphabet's board are also facing another shareholder action for unjust enrichment and corporate waste.[2] Data breaches also leave boards vulnerable, with shareholders bringing cases against the directors of Yahoo, Equifax, and Marriott International, to name but a few. While in February 2023, environmental law charity ClientEarth (supported by a group of pension funds and other institutional investors) filed a lawsuit against 11 directors on the board of Shell, claiming they had failed in their legal duty under the UK Companies Act to bring Shell's strategy in line with meeting the climate targets set out in the 2015 Paris Agreement.[3]

CEO and Senior Leadership Pressures

The relationship between a board and CEO isn't always an easy one. Not all CEOs are amenable to oversight by the board. High-profile leaders with an outstanding record for growing the company and delivering good shareholder returns can become untouchable, making it almost impossible for the board to do its job effectively. As a consequence, over time, board members can grow afraid of this type of CEO. In his candid description of his time as chairman of Nokia, Risto Siilasmaa recalls how difficult it was to dissent, or even to raise questions, in board meetings when he joined the board in 2008 chaired by Jorma Ollila, Nokia's superstar ex-CEO. "As just one person—and the most junior member—on the board of directors I felt an almost physical pain because I had neither the access nor the authority to instigate the kind of systematic, fact-finding deep dive that would have enabled me to understand what was happening and more importantly why it was happening." He goes on to say, "In many ways, we [board members] were all captives of our perception of our roles. . . . We trusted our Chairman . . . [and] believed that no matter how bad things looked, he was intimately involved with the management team and fixing the problems."[4]

What Siilasmaa describes is far from the exception. Whether through a lack of time, an adherence to the belief that a board's role is to "monitor," complete confidence in the vision and ability of the CEO and executive team, or fear of opposing them, it is clear that too few boards are prepared to challenge their firm's executive leadership. One suspects that had they done so at firms like GE, Boeing, or Nokia, for example, these companies would not have found themselves facing the crises they did.

Even when board members have private doubts, they may not be willing to voice them and risk being labeled as the troublemaker who upsets the status quo. Various studies have shown that humans are neurologically wired to adjust our opinions to fit with the group consensus.[5] Further, they will subconsciously change their views to do so.[6] This pressure to conform can be even stronger in elite business circles or small countries, where reputations can rapidly unravel, resulting in professional and social isolation. Take France, for example, where more so than in many countries, business leaders tend to come from a small number of elite universities and share the same professional patrons. For many years, Claude Bebear, ex-CEO and chair of AXA, exercised a disproportionate influence in CEO appointments at various companies. In an environment like this, speaking out against the consensus could be nothing short of professional suicide.

Setting aside any disposition toward conformity, it is very difficult and often ill-advised for directors to challenge the CEO and executive team when financial performance appears to be strong. So often after a crisis, boards are called to account for not having intervened sooner. But even if boards suspect internal problems exist, it takes a lot of courage to bring these issues to light because doing so could result in a near-term drop in the company's share price and reputation. Many of the firm's shareholders, to whom the board owes a duty of loyalty to protect their financial interests, would not be happy at the short-term losses they may incur as a result of internal weaknesses being made public by the board. It is so much easier for boards to be reactive to obvious problems that have found their way into the public domain than to expose potential problems themselves.

Expanding the Role and Responsibilities of the Board

It's worth remembering that the role of the board as we know it today originally came into being in the 1970s as the "agency" solution to deal with the separation of ownership and control. And this solution was an independent board that would monitor managers on behalf of diffuse shareholders—whereas prior to this, "advisory" boards had been part of the senior management team. Although there are different nuanced interpretations of the activities of the modern board, there is general agreement that the basic oversight and monitoring responsibilities include approving the corporate strategy; overseeing risk management; succession planning; approving financial reporting; approving divestments and acquisitions; agreeing on executive compensation; ensuring the company meets legal and regulatory standards; protecting company assets; and representing the interests of shareholders.[7] Significant parts of this work, of course, are undertaken by various committees—audit, compensation, nominating and governing standing committees, with the addition of ad hoc committees created to deal with specific issues as and when they arise.

Whether these basic responsibilities are any longer sufficient is open to debate. Although the two huge corporate scandals at the beginning of the millennium, Enron and WorldCom, ushered in a broader corporate governance mandate with the introduction of the Sarbanes–Oxley Act and Richard Breeden's influential report, *Restoring Trust*,[8] more recent scandals, such as the collapse of blood testing technology firm Theranos or the Volkswagen emissions case, have yet to lead to any action but have opened a new discourse about the role of boards. At the same time, the financial crisis, growing environmental and sustainability concerns, and increasing public distrust in corporations and their leaders have led to a clarion call that standards and practices of corporate governance have to change.

But change to what? Beyond the need for change, there seems to be little consensus about what the next stage in the evolution of boards and governance should look like. Some experts and commentators advocate strengthening the current board model by developing more rigorous performance metrics.[9] A common call is for dedicating more time to board activities.[10] Some propose bringing in more outside expert advisers.[11] Others suggest improving internal board processes.[12] There is a widespread belief that achieving greater gender diversity in board composition will result in better boards; focusing more on issues relating to risk and integrity is another option that has been raised.[13] And while most of these suggestions make sense, they fall short of providing a holistic proposal to deal with the many challenges facing companies today and in particular the growth curse.

That's not to say more radical suggestions haven't been made. A number of people have argued that the boards of listed companies would benefit from adopting many of the structures and practices of private equity (PE) boards.[14] Much smaller PE boards meet more regularly and dedicate a lot more time to board work. They have a much greater involvement in strategy and are frequently the source of strategic ideas. They also collaborate more closely with management, both formally and informally. PE boards are composed of active, mid-career professionals, and perhaps as one might expect in the world of PE finance, to align their own interests and motivation with that of the PE investor, directors have a large financial stake in the company of which they are a board member.

Undoubtedly, some aspects of the PE board model would help improve the quality of governance at listed companies, although the idea of a more-or-less wholesale adoption is flawed. With their diffuse and diverse shareholders, listed companies operate in a much more complex environment. They have greater responsibility to a wider range of stakeholders and need to take a longer-term view than the average four-year investment of PE firms.

Neither a piecemeal approach to improving certain aspects of board composition and activities nor a shift to a PE-type board model seem sufficient to deal with the challenges facing the governance of listed companies today (and particularly mature companies in disruptive environments). Instead, our research has led us to believe that the way forward is a model of governance in which the role of the board is not only expanded but, more importantly, becomes more strategic (figure 4.1 sketches the shift to this new model). And we would argue that with investors bringing more lawsuits against board members for what in essence are strategic failures at companies, then

Figure 4.1: A Model of Strategic Governance: The Board's Role

both directors and investors should want to see strategy taking on a greater role in the governance of companies.

As is clear in figure 4.1, the basics of good governance practice have to remain essential, and a more strategic role should not become a distraction from that discipline. But nonetheless, as part of its stewardship and duty to stakeholders, a good board has the ultimate responsibility for the robustness of the firm and its future. With this in mind, it becomes difficult to see how boards can perform their role in safeguarding a company effectively without the broadening of their mandate and having a stronger presence in the strategy process.

A Blueprint for an Effective Strategic Board

What follows are the eight core responsibilities and capabilities our research has led us to believe are essential for the board to be able to play a more strategic role. As with many proposals that have been put forward to improve the quality and scope of governance to reflect the challenges facing companies, the environment, and societies today, we recognize that parts of our manifesto would require certain regulatory changes—for instance, in relation to director independence (which is naturally challenged if boards are more strategic). However, as the status quo clearly isn't working effectively, perhaps something more than a tinkering at the edges is called for.

1. Strategic Direction

First, we need to differentiate between two basic layers of strategy making. One is the activity systems[15] and path toward better performance, which lies firmly within the purview of the CEO and executive team. The other, called variously the "central idea" by Ram Charan and his coauthors, the "strategy kernel" by Richard Rumelt, and "strategic intent" by Gary Hamel and C. K. Prahalad, is about identifying, articulating, and describing the underlying logic of a firm and its long-term ambition.[16] We are calling it the "strategic direction"—a broad-brush view of the strategy space a company should pursue in the long-term and with which the CEO's short- to mid-term strategy needs to be aligned.

It falls to the board to define and adapt the company's strategic direction, share it with the CEO and executive team, and ensure it is communicated to employees, shareholders, and other stakeholders. It's important that defining the strategic direction is the duty of the entire board and not a subcommittee because owning and understanding the strategic direction provides a foundation for so many other aspects of the board's core responsibilities.

Without an agreed-on strategic direction (particularly in times of disruption or maturity), strategy making risks becoming little more than a succession of short-term goals that fail to address the real challenges a company is facing—and as we saw in chapter 3, CEOs under pressure are unlikely to make the best long-term strategic decisions for a company. Added to this, in firms that have been very successful and achieved operational excellence, management's strategic sensitivity will be dulled to the extent that managers are unlikely to recognize inflection points that jeopardize the premise of their strategy. [17]

When the board owns the strategic direction of the firm, its role shifts from one of relative reactivity in merely approving the CEO's strategy to being much more proactive: For instance, having deeper knowledge, board members can ask more probing and critical questions about the CEO's strategy and whether it makes sense based on the strategic direction of the firm. As the custodians of the strategic direction, they can alert management to possible external risks and internal weakness. The board is also in a stronger position to collaborate with management to navigate the firm through significant change and renewal.[18] Finally, diversified companies run the risk of pursuing too many different goals given that business unit strategies and corporate value-adding strategies are different.[19] A better informed board responsible for the strategic direction of the overall firm can ensure resources are focused on strategic coherence across the portfolio.

2. Purpose

The board has to have a collective commitment to a shared ambition beyond strategy that defines the purpose for which the company exists and explains why the company's ambition is worthy of pursuit. Understanding and being committed to the company's purpose is vitally important because, like it or not, we live in a world where the collective management of finite resources calls for firms to express how they contribute to the planet's future and where society sees itself as giving firms a license to operate, even if implicitly. And as such, firms are under growing pressure from external stakeholders and also increasingly from their own employees to articulate, communicate, and be true to their purpose.

Due to the relentless operational and performance pressures facing management, it is easy to see how "purpose" might fall by the wayside in strategic decisions and the voices of sustainability and ethics officers go unheard. So the board has a critical role to play here as management's "conscience keeper," ensuring that the wider societal and environmental responsibilities of the corporation and its broader purpose remain in focus.

3. Buffering

Rather than amplify and transmit outside pressures to executive management—principally from analysts and shareholders—a responsible board should dampen and even absorb them. We saw in earlier chapters how the relentless pressure for short-term growth can lead to a range of misbehaviors that in fact hasten the demise of a company, particularly when that company is mature, has reached the growth plateau, and is lacking genuine new growth opportunities. To help avoid this, it is incumbent on the board to provide "air cover"—that is, to allow management to take a more detached perspective and focus on both managing the growth plateau and the company's renewal options rather than be constantly buffeted by the vagaries of a volatile stock market.

At the same time the board has to act as a buffer protecting executives from unrealistic investor demands, it also needs to protect shareholders by ensuring management actions are not being taken in order to enrich or benefit themselves at the expense of shareholders and other stakeholders.[20]

4. Probing

CEOs and senior executives often live in a bubble of good news with subordinates unwilling to raise thorny issues or highlight potential problems. And if executives are kept isolated from reality, they won't know what questions need asking in order to understand the true state of their company and their industry.[21] This is particularly true in mature, successful companies. So the board needs to step in and be responsible for helping management by asking the type of tough questions that force serious reflection and enable executives to identify problems. Probing will only be successful if the board keeps framing and reframing its questions to ensure the CEO and executive team take a systemic perspective and don't fall back on linear cause-and-effect relationships that tend to assign more rationality to situations and outcomes than is true. As we outlined in chapter 2, dealing with complexity is hard for executives, so the board needs to be vigilant about not letting them slip back into the comfort of simplistic thinking.

It is also important that when probing, directors do not proffer proposals or provide answers. This might undermine management authority, commitment, and accountability—after all, the directors are not there to replicate the work of the executive. It can also be fraught with risk because even with detailed knowledge of the company's strategy, board directors do not spend enough time on a regular basis in the companies they oversee to be omniscient.

5. Measuring

Boards must also develop and adopt meaningful performance metrics, pertinent to assessing not just current financial results (which is easy) but also the more strategic aspect of the company's potential (which is much more difficult to assess). For instance, earnings per share provide only a partial picture and may not be a good measure of longer-term health. And as we observed in chapter 3 they can easily be manipulated by management under pressure. To take another example, discounted cash flow projections are often heavily dependent on residual value. The longer the time horizon, the more uncertain residual value may become. This may discourage longer-term market creation strategies and innovations, as the false safety of shorter time horizons may seem preferable. By overly relying on well-used financial metrics, boards also run the risk of aligning themselves with the simple measurement criteria analysts use—buy, hold, or sell, essentially labeling a company as good or bad.

6. Risk Assessment

Just as it is important for boards to take a systems approach to deal with complexity when probing, it is also vital when assessing risk. The increase in global connectivity means complex system dynamics come into play much more than they ever used to; as such, small changes in tangentially related areas can have huge effects. And, for boards, that means they need to be able to constantly assess organizational resilience against these uncontrollable risks.[22] For instance, few companies give explicit attention to the unknown risks that stem from environmental conditions brought about by climate change. Although these risks might be difficult to anticipate, their impact on business can be devastating: In 2018, a serious drought in Germany resulted in BASF having to dramatically cut back production at the world's largest integrated chemical facility because the Rhine, the river on which the plant relies for shipping (supplies in and product out), was too low for barges to navigate it.[23] This unforeseen risk was not only significant for BASF, but it caused problems throughout the supply chain.

Although not every eventuality can be anticipated, it behooves boards to both make sure management is aware that improbable risks should not be discounted—as they can be the most damaging—and that risk assessment methods take complexity into account.

7. Talent Assessment

When a board has to gauge the strategic resilience of a company, the quality of the executive bench, one or two levels below the CEO, is perhaps one of the most important factors to consider. The idea that the CEO alone can drive corporate performance is fanciful, to say the least, as a company has too many complex relationships for one person to have such a big effect.[24] And it is often the people outside the C-suite—those closer to the action who are heading up businesses, functions, and regions—who have a clearer perspective on the underlying issues and competitive threats the company faces. Talking to this cadre of management will not only allow the board to understand the strengths and gaps in the company's talent pool, but it will also allow the board to tap a valuable source of knowledge about the firm.

8. Succession Planning

Understanding the talent a company has below the executive team is obviously also a huge advantage for the board when it comes to succession planning for the CEO role. Given that there is no evidence that outside hires perform any better than insiders, planning for smooth successions is critical, and when a board fails in this basic duty, the consequences can be very damaging. We discuss this in more detail in chapter 8.

■

To play a more active role in guarding against the growth curse and building solid foundations for a company's long-term viability for all stakeholders, the mandate of the board needs to change. And playing a much clearer and stronger role in the strategy process by taking ownership of the strategic direction of the firm is one of the biggest changes and challenges facing boards. Meeting and overcoming the challenges will call for boards that look and feel different—boards with the new skills, structures, and processes needed to make governance more strategic.

5 ■ Building an Effective Board

Despite the obvious importance of having an effective board, to date a rigorous set of principles and guidelines for building the optimal high-performance board has been lacking. To do this requires understanding what motivates successful people to become board members; what to look for to ensure each board member can contribute to the board's strategic role; the key traits, skills, and characteristics essential for the board to work well as a group; and how best to manage that group so that they work effectively with each other to maintain alignment between the CEO, executive team, shareholders, and various stakeholder groups in light of the company's long-term prosperity.

Director Motivation

If boards are to be effective in delivering the eight key contributions outlined in chapter 4, individual directors will not only need to be impartial and highly engaged, but they will have to bring no personal agenda to the role. Or, to think of it another way, the primary motivation for people to become board directors should be the desire to perform a type of public service by providing the best stewardship for the longevity of the company and for all stakeholders.[1] Wonderful though the idea is of having talented leaders selflessly dedicating themselves to director roles, in reality, human frailties mean that self-interest plays a large part in director motivation, whether it be for the prestige and networking, the compensation, using the position as a springboard to an executive role, vindication, or to make an impact:

> *Prestige and networking*—Successful people are often motivated to join boards because of the prestige and status a directorship can bring.[2] This is particularly the case when the position is at a highly visible and reputable company. What better way could there be to send a clear signal to colleagues, former colleagues, associates, or friends that you have been sought out to join a very small elite? And rather conveniently, directorships also provide a fantastic networking opportunity, which in turn can lead to more directorships and more networking! Obviously, when prestige and networking are one of the primary motivators for joining a board, this will be detrimental to the company, because directors who are overly concerned with their own self-image and self-interest will be inclined to act in whatever way is necessary to maintain their place

on the board. They are far from the selfless, impartial types needed for effective boards.

Compensation—Although compensation can play a role in the motivation to become a director, it's worth noting that the level of compensation and how it is divided between fees and shares varies dramatically by country. In the United Kingdom, for example, in 2021 the average annual fee for directors of companies listed on the FTSE 100 was £70,785.[3] This fee represents the major proportion of compensation as the UK Corporate Governance Code discourages compensation in shares on the basis that this diminishes director independence. In contrast, in the United States, the average director fee at S&P 500 firms is $136,133, but hefty additional equity payments take the total annual average compensation to a shade under $316,091.[4] In the eyes of many, this distracts the board from its true mission. It is difficult to see how directors can be independent when a large chunk of their compensation is aligned to the company's share price.

Even at the lower end of the director pay scale in countries like the United Kingdom, Sweden, and Italy, director fees are still attractive given the little time required for board business and the networking effect. Consequently, most directors hold multiple directorships. If pay ratios comparing director compensation with that of average employees were published, with hours actually worked factored into the equation, many directors would find themselves facing "excessive pay" attacks similar to those leveled against CEOs in recent years. Even though it is unlikely that the odd million dollars from a handful of directorships would be motivation to join boards for those CEOs whose compensation packages amount to tens of millions of dollars a year, for many people, it would prove very attractive spending money indeed.

For directors who are still working as executives in another company, there is an additional side to the motivation of compensation that is less obvious, as it is a second-order effect. Research involving over 2,000 senior executives at S&P 1500 firms found that serving on a board resulted in an increase in the executive's "day job" salary of around 13 percent.[5]

Springboard to a CEO role—Many up-and-coming executives see a nonexecutive director role as a good route for promotion to their first CEO appointment. In fact, the same study that found being a nonexecutive director had a positive impact on executive salaries also found that executives who served on boards were 44 percent more likely to be promoted into their first CEO position than their peers in similar roles at similar firms who didn't serve on boards.[6]

As far as executives who already have a CEO position or a high-profile executive management team role under their belt, some may be attracted to join the boards of companies, particularly those that are in trouble, in the belief that once on the inside, they stand a good chance of being appointed to the position of CEO. Many talented and successful executives, with a mindset not too different from that of an activist investor, would relish the opportunity to turn a company around one more time. It may well be that these individuals turn out to be the right

CEO for the company, having an understanding of the issues, the right skills for the role, and the backing of their former colleagues on the board.

Nonetheless, whether moving upward or sideways, seeing a directorship as a springboard to the CEO role is the wrong reason to join a board. Somewhat worryingly, recent data show that in US-listed companies, appointments of nonexecutive directors to the CEO role are in fact increasing—in 2020, representing 23 percent of "internal candidate" hires in Russell 3000 firms and 14.6 percent in S&P 500 companies.[7]

Vindication—Former CEOs may see director roles as a route to vindicate their convictions, replay their successes, or right their failures. This is a particular problem when director candidates have poorly healed scars from their executive career and may be unconsciously tempted to replay past actions that they felt were right but for which they did not receive much praise or recognition or, much worse, for which they were castigated or even fired. It is important to remember that just like managers, directors have history and bring their own personal heuristics and dominant logic to the role. But as directors, they should not be motivated to behave as if they were still on the executive team—they need to recognize the deeply different nature of the roles.

Making a difference—Here we have a genuine intrinsic motivation that is both good and true. After long and successful careers, some people are drawn to director roles simply because they want to have an impact on the future of a firm.[8] Furthermore, they enjoy working to chart that future without having to assume the operational responsibilities of an executive.

In sum, directors' motives can be quite varied, from the lofty to the grossly self-interested. But even with the right background and motivation, directors may not be up to the job simply because they are unable to dedicate the time needed to undertake the eight core responsibilities we outlined in chapter 4. There is a general consensus that to be effective requires directors to spend more time on board work. Add this to another frequently made suggestion that directors should have CEO experience—if only to understand governance challenges and board interactions from an executive standpoint—and it becomes even more difficult to find the best people to fill director roles who are available for enough time to devote strategic attention to the company's future.

What companies often find in their boards, then, is a bench of directors who are impressive on paper, yet because of other demands placed on them, they are incapable of dedicating the requisite amount of attention to the company boards they sit on. Looking at the board of Nokia back in the 2000s, a former director told us that Henning Kagermann (at the time, co-CEO of SAP) and Marjorie Scardino (then CEO of Pearson Group) could have both played a more active role on the Nokia board and provided strong and insightful checks and balances to Jorma Ollila's overbearing and mercurial style if they had been able to devote more time to Nokia's fortunes. A lack of time is not only about an individual's ability to make it to meetings fully prepared and engaged, but is also about the scheduling and agendas of those meetings. It is not unusual for boards to have 15 to 20 agenda items to work through in a four-hour meeting, and if anything related to long-term competitiveness is placed toward the end of the agenda, the implicit message is that it isn't that important.

With all of this in mind, it is imperative that the chair of the board understands the motivations of each director and can realistically assess not only their ability and interest in the role but also whether they have the time to be fully committed to safeguarding the future of the company.

The Importance of "Strategic Minds"

Regardless of what other skills, knowledge, and experience they bring to the table, directors have to be especially skilled strategists and in particular have "strategic minds" if they are to be effective guardians of the company's future as well as the owners of its strategic direction. Pekka Ala-Piettilä, one of the strategic minds behind Nokia's initial success in mobile phones in the 1990s, believes that "no one can be a board member without having a real understanding of strategy,"[9] and this understanding is deeper than the skills honed in strategy functions or as business heads. What makes a strategic mind is a combination of largely innate traits that bestow on an individual the ability to see the world differently from most others, question things that others don't recognize or take for granted, and make connections between seemingly disparate events and information in a way that new opportunities or threats come into focus.

There has been little prior research looking into what makes a strategic mind, but having observed and studied everything from great to good to mediocre strategists over many decades, we have put together what we believe are the key traits underlying a strategic mind:

Cognitive flexibility—We interpret the world through the lens of our experience, our surroundings, the prevailing norms, and their resulting mental frameworks. Cognitive flexibility is the skill to move beyond this context to recognize, interpret, synthesize, and see the significance of things that are cognitively distant, difficult to perceive, or unfamiliar—and then discover and explore relatedness and linkages between these distant facts or observations.

Nonlinear thinking—Linear or sequential thinking is vital for effective operations—it allows you to get from A to Z via a defined set of steps. But studies have shown that nonlinear approaches, such as systems thinking or associative thinking, produce more creative outcomes.[10] It is this type of thinking we find in strategic minds. To some extent, everyone uses associative thinking, as we intuitively make sense of the world by making an association between the unfamiliar and our past experience, but people with strategic minds are much more open than most and are likely to be able to consciously "free associate," linking up multiple inputs with existing knowledge.[11] They don't see the world in a simple linear way but as a series of complex interlinking systems where small changes can result in dramatic effects.[12]

Handling ambiguity—Most people are uncomfortable with ambiguity, preferring clarity and a vision of the future in which little change is required because this enables them to retain a sense of control.[13] Not so people with a strategic mind—they have a high tolerance for ambiguity that is found in competing points of view, contradictory inputs, and complexity. They understand that ambiguity is a fact and control is illusory, and so they remain open to multiple hypotheses about the changes they perceive.

Willingness to tackle hard problems—Perhaps resulting from their cognitive flexibility, nonlinear thinking, and openness to ambiguity, people with strategic minds do not shy away from difficult problems, nor do they attempt to simplify difficult problems. In contrast, most managers avoid hard problems, and when they can't be avoided, they resort to "cognitive simplification."[14] That is, they use a set of heuristics they have learned over their careers to break down problems so that they can apply existing hypotheses.

Big picture—Strategic minds are intuitively more drawn to and influenced by the big picture than isolated events.[15] As such, they cultivate a wide set of relationships both inside and outside the company. In a sense, they are the modern equivalent of the polymaths of old, seeking out knowledge and understanding across multiple different disciplines and fields.

Consummate questioners—As we progress through education and the rungs of corporate hierarchies, we are trained to provide answers. Asking questions, after all, can be seen as a weakness, singling one out as failing to understand something that the brighter, cleverer people grasp. While Hal Gregersen's work on the importance of asking questions brought the idea of question brainstorming into vogue,[16] people with strategic minds have always stood apart from the throng of executives armed with ready answers. Led by their inquiring minds, they ask questions to broaden their understanding, challenge potential biases, and help others see new threats and opportunities.

Mindfulness and sense-making—To the strategic mind, the journey is never complete. There is a strong awareness that ideas and assumptions need to be continually challenged and refined as new knowledge or experience comes into play.[17] But merely being highly perceptive isn't enough—abstract ideas and perceptions have to be translated into actionable frameworks that make sense to the rest of the organization.[18] In other words, meaning has to be attached.

Self-awareness—It would be unusual to find a person with a truly strategic mind who was also narcissistic or hungry for power. The very essence of having a strategic mind means actively seeking to challenge one's worldview and assumptions and thus one's own identity and power—something that is anathema to most managers.[19] It takes a high level of self-awareness to be able to continually and openly question, and potentially undermine, the context within which you operate and not fall victim to the dominant logic of a company. Self-awareness is also critical in getting others on board with new directions or ideas, particularly when dealing with defensive CEOs in successful, mature companies.

Getting Board Composition Right

To recap, if companies are to avoid the short-termism of the growth curse, governance has to be more strategic. This means carrying out the core responsibilities of the board that we proposed in chapter 4, which can only be done effectively if having a strategic mind is a prerequisite for all board members. But there are five other attributes that play a critical role in building effective boards—cognitive diversity, deep and broad knowledge, industry experience, board size, and length of tenure—each of which we will now discuss.

Cognitive Diversity

In recent years, diversity has been one of the buzzwords around board composition. And this makes sense at the broader level as a lack of diversity can lead to a board that finds it easy to discuss matters but risks falling victim to groupthink—negating the value of any dialogue. But the types of diversity that have dominated the headlines are not necessarily the best for building board effectiveness. At the risk of trampling over political correctness, while gender diversity on boards is undoubtedly good for society, studies have shown that it has little or no impact on company performance.[20] And cultural diversity, the other flag bearer of balanced boards, can make it difficult to sustain real dialogues because individual directors lack common reference points and may even lack a common language beyond the basics of "business speak."

What is more rarely discussed but is in fact the most important type of diversity for board effectiveness is cognitive diversity—the differences in how people process information and solve problems, allowing different perspectives to be brought to the table. It is these differences that lead cognitively diverse teams to perform much better, particularly in uncertain and complex situations.[21] Provided there are shared norms of problem solving—in other words, agreement and commonality on group processes when facing difficult issues—cognitively diverse boards benefit from the richness of multiple perspectives yet retain the ability to function as a team.

Of course, cognitive, gender, and cultural diversity are not mutually exclusive, so there may be some overlap. However, the anchor of board diversity should be cognition, and if that results in gender and cultural diversity too, then all the better.

Deep and Broad Knowledge

Boards also need to have the right balance between deep knowledge and diverse knowledge. In boards, like elsewhere, T-shaped skills are highly desirable. Yet the more diversified a firm is, the more challenging it becomes to balance deep expert knowledge and experience (the vertical bar of the T) with an ability to understand, appreciate, and be critical of other people's expertise and contributions (the horizontal bar). Too much similarity in depth and individual contributions can become redundant; not enough breadth, and mutual understanding is lost. So the question has to be asked: Does each director bring depth in one particular area and enough breadth of knowledge to relate usefully to other directors and contribute to a collective team process?

A good example of a board that lacked diverse knowledge was the group of luminaries brought together to serve as directors for the now-defunct blood testing technology firm Theranos. The Theranos board included two former secretaries of state, a former secretary of defense, two former senators, a former general, and a former admiral—perhaps a little limiting for a medical technology company? What's more, they were all white males with an average age of 76.[22] The Theranos board not only lacked the deep medical or technology expertise that was critical to the company's activities, but it failed in terms of relevant diverse knowledge, too. It is hardly surprising, then, that the board didn't spot the underlying inaccuracies and problems that led to the collapse of the company.

Industry Experience

Just as with knowledge, "deep and diverse" should be the mantra when thinking about the industry experience individual directors bring to the board. Directors who have a mix of deep and diverse experience have a greater influence on strategy making because they aren't confined to a silo and can see areas of opportunity and threat from convergence across industries.[23]

Having some directors who have relevant industry experience relating to the firm can help with monitoring the firm's strategic position, as their expertise allows them to notice anomalies in firm performance that people less familiar with the industry might not detect.[24] And having directors who serve on the boards of other companies in related fields brings the advantage of widening the board's understanding of developments and trends in a firm's operating markets, environment, or ecosystem.[25] This is particularly important in industries that are experiencing transformation and in fast-moving sectors—something that is reflected in the fact that the boards of technology companies tend to have more industry experts on them than boards in other sectors.[26]

And in mature companies whose growth is stalling, rather than appointing well-known names from other large, mature companies to the board, it makes sense to bring in new directors with experience in high-growth industries to add a few explorers to the farmers.

Board Size

Beyond the attributes of the individuals best suited to contribute as team members of the board, the actual size of the board also matters and has an impact on a board's effectiveness. As we touched on in chapter 4, one of the characteristics of private equity boards which is believed to contribute to their success is their relatively small size. According to executive search firm Spencer Stuart, "A board needs to be large enough to allow for a wide range of views and competencies and for each of the committees to be populated, but not so large as to prevent active engagement and participation by all directors. . . . When boards move into double figures they become less effective: it is harder to sustain effective debate when numerous people are at the table."[27]

A survey commissioned by the *Wall Street Journal* found that small boards delivered greater returns for investors as better dynamics meant they were able to discuss, debate, and drill down to details much more successfully than larger boards.[28] Conventional wisdom puts the ideal size of a board for a large, publicly listed company at between seven and eight members—more than this and it's difficult for boards to be hands-on, and some individual directors will become less attentive and less involved.

Length of Tenure

Length of tenure is another critical factor of board composition, and it is one that throws up difficult trade-offs. Long-serving directors may not necessarily be best placed to provide the foresight and imagination needed to chart a future direction for a company, particularly in the face of firm maturity, external disruption, or industry transformation. They may well be out of touch with developments in the industry and emerging competitive threats. For instance, in the United States, where term limits for directors are rare[29] (around 5 percent of S&P 500 companies have term-limit policies), the average tenure for non-executive directors is a shade under 10 years, and around one-sixth of directors currently serving have been in their post for at least 16 years.[30] With so many entrenched positions, is continuity likely to be favored over change? Although these legacy directors may be hard to remove when CEOs and the board chair control the appointment of directors, they are less likely to survive proxy contests brought by shareholders wishing to see greater diversity in the team that represents their interests.

On the other hand, long-serving directors have their benefits. They have a good understanding of the pattern of interpersonal interactions within the board, they are likely to be trusted by other board members, and they possess a deeper understanding of the company they represent.

New directors can come with their own limitations. For a start, becoming an effective director does not happen overnight. It is likely to take time for new directors to understand the intricacies of the company and build credibility with their fellow board members and executives. Yet they can also bring clear advantages, particularly in times of disruption. Not being imbued with a company's orthodoxies means they can offer a fresh perspective to challenges and opportunities and may be able to tap different networks to recognize powerful trends in the industry ahead of competitors.

So there are merits to both board continuity and renewal, calling for a balancing act that staggered boards (with directors elected to a three-year term and reelections staggered so that only a third of director seats are up for reelection each year) can provide a good solution to meeting. Opponents of staggered boards believe they do not serve shareholders well, as it takes two years (instead of one round of voting) for proxy contests to be successful (and activists to take control of the board). Supporters, on the other hand, argue that staggered boards protect shareholders from opportunistic, hostile takeovers and provide stability. It is worth noting that in the United States at least, trends for staggered boards paint an equally divided picture: 41 percent of S&P 500 companies used staggered boards in 2009, but the number declined to only 10 percent in 2021. However, almost 41 percent of companies in the much broader Russell 3000 Index were using staggered boards in 2021.[31]

Leadership Unity within the Board

So far in this chapter, as shown in figure 5.1, we have looked at the motivations and skills needed for individual directors and

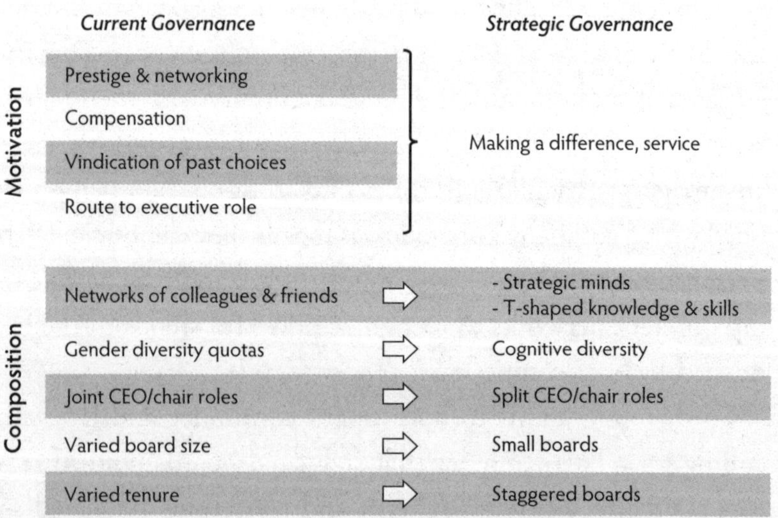

Figure 5.1: A Model of Strategic Governance: Motivation and Composition

how they should be combined. Now we move on to what's needed to bring the right individuals together to create the optimal board for meeting the challenges of company longevity, environmental sustainability, and societal good in an increasingly complex world. This involves group work achieved through unity, an effective chair, and regular assessment.

Board Unity

In a discussion about board effectiveness with Sydney Finkelstein (who has many years of experience advising boards and has conducted research with hundreds of directors), he told us that he had found "boards are not teams in any meaning of the term; they are [individual] free agents often with different goals."[32] Sadly, the numerous board members, board coaches, executive search specialists, consultants, and academics we spoke with during the course of our research for this book generally concur with Sydney. Unity is not a common facet of most boards, and they rarely function as a group working toward shared goals.

Yet it is critical that all directors are able to work together. And to illustrate the key elements to achieving this, we are borrowing from the strategic agility framework originally put forward by Yves Doz and Mikko Kosonen in their 2008 book *Fast Strategy*.[33] At the heart of this framework is the idea that the agility needed for continual renewal comes from strong capabilities in three vectors: leadership unity, strategic sensitivity, and resource fluidity (which we will discuss in more detail in chapter 10). Although the concepts of strategic agility were developed with executive management in mind, we have come to realize that many of the lessons are equally applicable to the functioning of effective strategic boards. And for the current discussion, we will look at what is needed to achieve the leadership unity required for a board of directors to work effectively together.

Dialogue—Essential to achieving unity in any group, dialogue involves open and honest discussion without fear of losing face or retaliation. There is no place for big egos in a true dialogue, and the goal is not to win an argument but for the board to converge around an agreed point of view. It doesn't matter what tools the board may use to support dialogues as long as the outcome is a collective commitment to the decision and the decision process.

Good and thoughtful dialogue will be much easier when the composition of the board is aligned with the attributes that we covered earlier. The questioning nature, cognitive flexibility, and self-awareness of individuals with strategic minds naturally draws them to dialogue. When each director brings broad and deep knowledge to the board, this favors the mutual respect needed for successful dialogue. And it is much easier to have meaningful discussions and to coalesce around an agreed point of view when you have a smaller board.

Revealing—This is about making the underlying motives of each director visible in relation to every dialogue the board embarks on. It's about putting any cognitive biases, ambitions, and concerns each individual may have on the table. Revealing is an important practice for making everyone feel secure about contributing fully to board dialogues. And the resulting culture of honesty and openness within the board puts a stop to second-guessing, speculation, and game playing. It also allows the board to explore ideas that may never have come to light without the sense of comfort and unity brought about through revealing.

Aligning—It is critical that the board rallies around common interests, compelling missions, shared values, and a keen sense of purpose. The board has to be aligned to present a united face both to the executive management and the investment community.

Empathizing—Being compassionate and able to empathize with others is important for group dynamics. It fosters a deeper level of understanding and helps build trust between individual directors.

Without leadership unity, boards are as vulnerable as any other group to the emergence of cliques and subgroups forming around charismatic and convincing individuals. Studies have shown that informal social networks outside official company business (whether from interlocking board appointments, old friendships, or shared interests) play a significant role in determining where decision-making power resides within boards. These social ties result in "inner boards" developing, the members of which are much less likely to dissent from the inner board's consensus opinion. And the arguments and thoughts of those directors who are not part of the inner board are unlikely to be heard.[34]

Boards that lack leadership unity cannot be effective, and activist shareholders understand this better than most. Strong activist pressure can divide boards—particularly when an activist has a seat on the board. We have heard anecdotal evidence that when activist-appointed board members lobby the board, meetings become acrimonious, loyalties are split, and the board can disintegrate into warring factions. Interestingly, the growth in passive index fund ownership of listed companies is likely to exacerbate the divisions in board unity caused by activists. There is evidence that when passive fund shareholding is higher, activists are more likely to focus on gaining board seats to try and steer the agenda of the board.[35]

The proliferation of committees can also accentuate the clique or subgroup risk within boards by creating knowledge asymmetries between directors and inevitably making some better informed and more influential than others, depending on which subcommittee(s) they sit. So, although subcommittee specialization may be a necessary solution to getting through the work of a board, bear in mind that subcommittees may also have a side effect of working against the leadership unity needed for collective commitment.

Another source of subgroup dynamics that threatens the leadership unity of the board arises from interactions between individual directors and executive management. One-on-one meetings between directors and a strong CEO, useful as they are, run the risk of undermining collective board processes and transforming the board into a series of bilateral relationships between individual directors and the CEO—which clearly puts the CEO in a position of control while weakening board unity.

An Effective Chair

A number of seasoned directors have told us that perhaps the most critical factor in determining the effectiveness of a board comes down to the skills and ability of its chair. The responsibility for setting both the agenda for board work and the culture of behavior within the board rests with them. Good chairs don't play political games or bring their own personal agenda to the role.[36] Much has been written about what it takes to be a good board chair.[37] So, rather than reinvent the wheel, we will outline some of the critical skills we believe contribute to effective board leadership.

Chairs have to encourage open dialogue and ensure everyone is heard. They foster collaboration within the board and between the executive and the board. They are the consummate diplomats: calm, unflappable, and rational at all times (even when facing a crisis). They are approachable, and they are clear that even though it may not be the easy thing to do, it is important to always do the right thing. When a skilled chair sets the tone of transparency, honesty, and modesty, a much better board will emerge.

It's difficult to discuss the effectiveness of board chairs without touching on the thorny issue of joint CEO/board chair roles. While for the most part this arrangement is the exception rather than the rule in most European companies, it is still common in the United States—though steadily declining. In 2005, 70 percent of S&P 500 CEOs were also chairs of the board, whereas by 2022, this number had fallen to 44 percent.[38] Although it is inconclusive whether separation of the roles affects a company's financial performance, most governance experts argue for separation to avoid conflicts between those monitoring and those being monitored across a number of areas, including compensation, succession planning, performance evaluation, and short-term gains versus long-term strategic perspectives.[39]

And you don't have to look very far to find examples of joint roles leading to significant problems. At Lehman Brothers, for instance, prior to its collapse in 2008, joint CEO and Chairman Dick Fuld had complete control over a board whose members, according to the *Financial Times*, "neither delved deeply enough into the real activities of the bank, nor did they challenge the person running it sufficiently."[40] In essence, as both Lehman's CEO and chair, Fuld was held accountable to no one, and as long as the bank's financial results appeared to be good, no one questioned the underlying strength of the business and its strategy.

We have heard anecdotal evidence of executives who will only accept CEO roles if they are chair of the board, too—the logic being that having both roles gives them an "insurance policy." This type of reasoning should certainly set alarm bells ringing. And given the heavy workload of CEOs, it is difficult to imagine that someone fully engaged with that role would have the time and capacity to do both the CEO and chair roles justice.

For different reasons, another troubling variant of the joint roles practice is when a retiring CEO becomes chair of the board. In this scenario, the new chair is likely to remain intellectually locked into their previous strategy and corporate development path as well as being emotionally attached to their past achievements. They believe in the direction in which they took the company and also want to defend their record. In fact, research has shown that when a former CEO is retained to chair the board, it has a stifling effect on the new CEO's ability to change strategy and results in a continuation of similar performance.[41] In other words, a former CEO becoming the board chair is likely to become a source of strategic inertia.

Board Assessment

Formal performance assessments of the kind managers undergo annually have not been that common at the board level. However, more chairs are finding it increasingly useful to bring in consultants to assess how the board functions as a team and undertake 360-degree type evaluations of the contributions of each individual board member.[42] While reviews of this kind are undoubtedly useful in bringing to light potential problems with group processes and dynamics and highlighting the strengths and gaps in individual capabilities needed for the current operating environment, they fall short in evaluating the board's ability to work effectively in the face of emerging discontinuities and disruption.

Industry transformation, complexity, or environmental change can seriously undermine the ability of directors to steer the company's strategic direction, as their own individual capabilities and knowledge bases may no longer be relevant. Continual self-assessment of the relevance of the capabilities, knowledge, and networks within the board against the changing external landscape would help bolster the legitimacy of boards as the architects of a company's long-term strategic direction. But beware. If individual directors have joined boards for the wrong reason—and here we need to loop back to our discussion of motivation earlier in this chapter—self-interest may well trump the importance of self-evaluation, and a company could end up facing organizational stagnation if its directors are not equipped to guide it through turbulent change.[43]

■

The damaging actions of executives in response to shareholder demands for short-term financial performance have gone unchecked in many firms for far too long as boards have sat on the sidelines focusing on their monitoring and oversight mandates. It makes no sense whatsoever that the ultimate custodians of a company have been largely absent from actively securing its future. Yet a board composed of people with the right motivations, strategic minds, and diverse yet complementary capabilities and knowledge—and especially when working as a team under the leadership of an impartial and skilled chair—will be able to make a genuine contribution to overcoming the growth curse and contributing to the strategy process in a meaningful way to protect the long-term interests of the firms they serve.

6 ■ Defining the Strategic Direction

Looking to the Future

If boards are to evolve to play a more active role in safeguarding the long-term future of companies and avoiding the growth curse, then a more strategic form of governance is key. With the average CEO tenure at around five to six years in most regions, we can hardly expect executive leadership to have the time or motivation to factor a long-term perspective into their strategies. And so, as we outlined in chapter 4, it should rightly fall to the board to set the strategic direction of the firm—the longer-term ambition.

For many boards, taking on the responsibility for defining a firm's strategic direction will at first seem way out of their comfort zones and perhaps beyond their capabilities. A McKinsey survey found that only 10 percent of directors believed they understood the dynamics of the industry of their firms.[1] This situation begs the question: If you don't have a good understanding of the players, value chain, ecosystems, potential areas of convergence, markets, technology trajectory, displacement threats, or regulatory issues of the industry in which the company you oversee operates, then how can you possibly be equipped to safeguard the future of that firm and define its long-term strategic direction? And how can directors gain the requisite knowledge and insight essential to fulfill their roles effectively in the limited time they have available for board work?

Recent research has confirmed that boards need to be able to develop strong insights into the environment in which their companies operate to support long-term value creation.[2] Not only are these insights crucial for setting the strategic direction, but they can arm the board with the understanding needed to alert the company's management to possible inflection points (whether they are shifts in technology, customer preferences, or market changes), which could derail the current strategy. They also give the board a strong foundation against which to scrutinize the CEO's strategy as well as the corporate coherence of the company's portfolio of businesses (more on that in chapter 9).

Strategic Sensitivity: Looking Outside to Imagine the Future

Recall from chapter 5 the three vectors of the strategic agility framework (leadership unity, strategic sensitivity, and resource fluidity) and how leadership unity is crucial if the board is to work as a team. Well, the vector of strategic sensitivity is just as important for directors, as a strong capability here will help the board be more aware of and alert to impending trends in the outside world that will affect and shape how they define the strategic direction.

Heightened strategic sensitivity first calls for superior anticipation and greater foresight that are gained from looking outside the firm. But just like management, boards are liable to take too much of an inside view. One consistent message that has come across from every governance expert and board member we spoke with is that boards operate in the here and now and do not focus on forecasting what challenges or opportunities the future may hold. Particularly in mature, successful companies, it is not unusual for board members and executive management to succumb to the same creeping cognitive biases largely based on past achievements.

For directors to break free from these biases and gain greater strategic sensitivity is not as difficult and onerous a task as one might expect. Clearly, some additional time commitment is needed to sift through inputs, analyze findings, and develop a shared point of view. But in terms of gathering the information, insights, and data, it is likely that many of the tools and methods that aim to understand the future trends integral to strategic sensitivity are already in use in the company's research and innovation units, and some may already be used by senior management as part of their strategy process.

Without attempting a comprehensive coverage or detailed treatment of these tools (each would deserve a whole chapter in a strategy textbook), instead we will provide a brief overview of the most important ones for the board to consider using for its own "strategic direction" deliberations. It's worth noting that the insight gained from these tools will also help the board have a better understanding of how good the CEO's strategy really is in addressing future trends and challenges.

Corporate Foresight Methods

Corporate foresight has its origins in the work of two individuals working independently of each other in the 1950s. In France, philosopher and manager Gaston Berger promoted a future-oriented approach to help companies and policy makers deal with complexity. While at the RAND Corporation in the United States, Herman Khan was developing scenario planning as a tool for the US military. Toward the end of the 1960s, it was another Frenchman, Pierre Wack, working for Royal Dutch Shell in London, who introduced and developed scenario decision planning as a corporate foresight tool for the first time. It wasn't long before the value of his work became apparent when the global energy crisis that Wack's group had anticipated in a 1972 scenario came to pass.

The purpose of corporate foresight is to develop a set of "what if" scenarios based on likely future challenges and opportunities arising from emerging trends, discontinuities, and disruptions across different geographies and a range of areas including politics, economics, demographics, technology, social changes, as well as specific industry insights. Shell's scenarios approach, for example, not only highlighted potential shifts direct to the oil industry but also foresaw indirect impacts such as the fall of the Soviet Union and the rise of Muslim radicalism.

The first step to building corporate foresight to support strategic sensitivity is the continual and systematic scanning or "sensing" of the external environment for weak signals and emerging discontinuities. The second step involves evaluating and plotting how these various findings might contribute to different possible futures. This process is supposed to challenge directors, and to ensure that it doesn't become hostage to their mindsets, it needs to involve a range of external experts and internal participants from different levels of the organization.

Making these possible futures specific to a firm's strategic direction also requires an awareness of the barriers that are likely to be encountered; otherwise, you end up with a long-term strategic direction that is little more than wishful thinking. Orthodoxies, for example, at both the firm and industry level are a particular problem because, over time, they become unchallengeable beliefs that can easily derail good foresight work unless they are identified and openly challenged. Similarly, sources of inertia to any potential futures, such as culture, corporate structures, or weak strategic assets, also need to be identified as early as possible because they are difficult and slow to change.

Since Shell's first incursions in the world of corporate scenario planning, the field of corporate foresight has grown both in the number of different tools and techniques available and the consultants specializing in employing them. Another approach initially developed by the RAND Corporation for military use in the 1950s, the now widespread Delphi method, for instance, seeks to reach an expert consensus on likely future outcomes through the anonymous responses of experts to questionnaires. After answers are collated, they are shared among the group before a new round of questions are asked, and this process continues. According to the RAND Corporation, "The goal is to reduce the range of responses and arrive at something closer to expert consensus."[3] In the 1980s, roadmaps supporting both innovation and strategy in the telecom and auto industries were developed, and the following decade this method was adopted more widely in the form of technology roadmaps.

None of these tools, however, is perfect. The data collected can be inaccurate, and interpretations of findings are obviously subjective. So the most robust corporate foresight comes from combining the outcomes of different techniques.[4]

Anticipating Disruptions and Inflection Points

When you are in the thick of it, it can feel as if major changes and disruptions hit you suddenly. But, in fact, they are rarely bolts out of the blue, and so having the ability and processes in place to anticipate potential disruptions forms an important tool in the armory of strategic sensitivity. Although this example is perhaps a little long in the tooth, the industry shift from video rental to content streaming illustrates the devastating results of missed inflection points and disruption. Anyone visiting the small town of Bend, Oregon, might be surprised to see a Blockbuster store with its once ubiquitous blue and yellow logo. At one time, Blockbuster dominated an industry with over 9,000 stores worldwide, but its demise was rapid when it was decimated by technology and business model innovations it failed to grasp.

Blockbuster's board and executive management should have been able to anticipate these innovations would change the face of movie home rentals. As early as 2001, Blockbuster had experimented with a video-on-demand service but abandoned this venture because it didn't fit with its brick-and-mortar store format and lucrative late-fee revenue model. In the meantime, Netflix, with its lower cost base and central distribution center, could offer customers a wider range of titles on DVD delivered by mail and on a subscription basis, eliminating late fees. As customers migrated to Netflix's by-mail and then later its streaming services, Blockbuster saw the changes taking place in the industry but resolutely stuck to its costly, outdated business model until it was too late. It's interesting to note that having been the disrupter, by 2020, Netflix and its subscriber, original content, and gaming business model was coming under strain from the advertiser-based model of YouTube. Whether Netflix's announcement in the final quarter of 2022 that it would start offering lower-priced subscriptions that include advertisements will be enough to stem its decline remains to be seen.

Major forces of disruption usually take up to 20 years to have an impact, particularly when they trigger multiple related changes over a broad front. So the issue for the board to consider is more often one of when and where rather than whether disruption will have an impact and, of course, how significant the consequences will be.

While it should be possible for boards to anticipate the primary impacts of disruption—for instance, that the choice and convenience of streaming movies would eventually displace rental stores for Blockbuster or that the arrival of digital photography would obliterate not only film sales but the processing of film for Kodak—secondary effects are more difficult to anticipate. To take a striking case, the driver behind Nokia's introduction of the first camera phone with picture-sharing applications was to encourage customer-generated content to help Nokia move from voice to mobile multimedia while circumventing the control of media content companies. This heralded a disruption in the mobile communications sector, but what wasn't obvious at the time was the secondary effect it would have—namely, it led to the "selfie" craze and ultimately drove the popularity and growth of Facebook, Instagram, and other social media firms.

Paying attention to innovations, technological trends, and diffusion cycles should help a board be better placed to anticipate their impact—positive or negative—and their timing. A word of warning, though: As the Gartner hype cycle illustrates, we are all vulnerable to the phenomena of hype, disappointment, and skepticism. There is initial excitement about an emerging technology or concept that increases with high-profile early successes. However, as problems and limitations become apparent, we become disillusioned and readily write off the idea and move on to the potential "next big thing," where the cycle starts over. It is important that boards do not become victims of the hype cycle, because some of the dismissed technologies will, of course, go on through various iterations of development and funding to indeed become the next big thing.

Boards cannot afford to dismiss potential disruptions just because experiments they are aware of have failed. The experiences of two Baby Bell companies, Bell South and US West, provide a salutary tale of how contrasting approaches to developing a nascent mobile communications business led to very different outcomes and therefore assessments of the prospects of this emerging sector. During the early days of wireless technology, full of energy and excitement, business unit staff at Bell South decided to adopt a growth and market share strategy. Promising early results reinforced the strategy, and continued growth strengthened the track record of the new business, resulting in senior managers being willing to allocate more resources to the fledgling business. Over at US West, meanwhile, based on the small potential market and high cost of the technology (back then we were talking brick-sized car phones for the very rich), a more conservative team had opted for a "cream skimming" strategy. Results for the first couple of years were worse than expected, so senior corporate managers lost faith and didn't allocate resources to this new disruptive technology.

People, energy, and context all contribute to whether a sufficient strategic commitment is made to developing disruptive businesses,[5] and the outcomes of experiments and new ventures need to be assessed in light of these internal factors. If you had only been assessing the potential disruption of mobile communications based on the case of US West, then you would have missed one of the biggest disruptions in the telecoms industry until it was too late.

However, broad assessments and an awareness of incipient trends and discontinuities, useful as they are, may not suffice alone. A deeper and more detailed technology scanning approach is often needed.

Technology Scanning

If put on the spot, few directors would be able to sketch with any certainty what their industry or business might look like 10 years from now. Yet, most of the technologies that will have a shaping influence on everything from banking to transportation in this 10-year time frame probably already exist in embryonic form, if not in their infancy. So, to set a compelling and value-creating strategic direction, one must have strategic sensitivity about emerging technologies and understand the array of future technologies and the impact they may have on your business and industry. Because these emerging technologies are likely to be dispersed geographically and across a dynamic range of diverse industries, you also need to build a specific capability to prospect from a huge and constantly changing pool.

One solution is to assign dedicated prospectors whose role is to act as "roving ambassadors," building networks of external contacts in fields that are likely to appear on your emerging technology radar. This is exactly what the US family-controlled steel and bearings producer, the Timken Company, did. Timken has long been a technological leader in its bearings business and produces some of the highest-quality precision bearings in the world for use in everything from jet engines to modern wind farms.

Timken's technology prospecting unit begins its journey by establishing liaisons with the group's research staff to identify broad complementary and disruptive technology domains. They then identify who and where experts are in a given field before setting out to talk to the people developing the technology and gaining a "feel" for it. From here, a "people trail" begins by asking the initial set of experts to tell them who they talk to when they face a problem, and this invariably leads to a core cluster of experts dispersed around the world. For example, when Timken was looking at microelectromechanical systems (MEMS), their search began at Berkeley and Cornell. Talking to people in these two universities and asking them who they turn to for input quickly revealed there was a very strong cluster of MEMS experts in Sweden—perhaps not the first place you would associate with this type of leading-edge technology.

Back at Timken's innovation center, as a check to confirm the newness of findings, the prospecting unit runs them by the business heads. If the business heads can instantly recognize the potential of new technologies, then the technology is too mature, and Timken is probably too late.

This type of technology scanning only works with the right type of people in the role. As Ken English, who established Timken's prospecting unit, explained, "They have to be respected within the organization to play the 'heretic,' to bat on the side of the long term."[6] And while these prospectors need to be able to absorb and interpret new technological knowledge, they also need the skills to communicate and build relationships and trust with people from dozens of different cultures around the world.

Listening to Customers

Listening to customers is undoubtedly an important input for good strategic sensitivity and for painting a picture of the current state of play and likely near-term (though not distant) future needs and trajectories. There are, however, limits to the usefulness of customers providing input to help define the strategic direction of a firm.

Most of us—not just customers—find it difficult to imagine or visualize a different technological trajectory or business model to the one we are invested in. While incremental improvements are seen as desirable and essential, customers will rarely want, demand, or expect a major discontinuity. Before he launched the Model T, Henry Ford is quoted as saying, "If I had asked people what they wanted, they would have said faster horses."

Instead of asking customers what they want in longer-term time horizons, a better place to start may be to investigate customer pain points—what really hurts them, or what they struggle with based on what is currently available to meet their needs. But even this has its limitations, and you can find yourself becoming hostage to your best customers even though they may not be representative of possible new future demand. So, for example, had Xerox asked its customers in the large central printing departments that bought licenses to make copies on expensive Xerox machines about their unmet needs, it's unlikely any would have identified a requirement for the small desktop copiers that Canon developed for the cramped office spaces of small enterprises in Japan. And yet it was these very machines from Canon that ultimately challenged Xerox's market dominance. So potential customers can be a more valuable source of ideas than existing ones.

Forward-Looking Indicators

Forward-looking indicators can be difficult to identify in the face of high uncertainty—and everything from political upheaval to pandemics and environmental sustainability makes it that much harder to recognize indicators that might help to paint a picture of a firm's future opportunities and challenges.

An approach to circumvent this difficulty is to rely on an array of change, discontinuity, and disruption scenarios, based on the outcomes of corporate foresight work and technology scanning. Looking at the path each scenario outlines, it should be possible to identify potential early changes, preconditions, and enabling conditions to these scenarios, which can then be used in the spirit of "time zero events"—in other words, as early-warning signals likely to trigger a set of deeper changes. These may be regulatory changes, technological innovations that are moving toward industrialization and diffusion (think next-generation batteries for electric vehicles), significant changes in customer behavior or customer demographics.

There are two useful things the board can do with these sets of indicators. First, review them regularly. They won't provide a crystal-ball view of the future, but they will keep the board's attention focused on potential future events, that without context (the scenarios), might otherwise be overlooked or dismissed.

Obviously, there is a cost to this approach, and there will be errors—some events will never materialize, and others may prove harmless. But it is better to identify and track these indicators than fall victim to a serious event triggering a major disruption for which the firm is not prepared. Second, use these indicators as part of an audit to assess the quality of the short- to mid-term strategic thinking of the CEO and executive team. The executive team should also be using the results from the range of foresight tools and processes to inform their strategic thinking and activity systems.

Learning Experiments

Although learning experiments may at first seem a little too close to the current strategy to be of use to the board's own long-term strategic mandate, they can in fact prove very informative in helping define a longer-term perspective.

In 1998, Sony introduced its first prototype robot in Japan—an electronic pet dog the company called AIBO—and the following year, Sony launched a consumer model. Bear in mind, even for early technology adopters, this was a leap because the world's first camera phone was still over a year away from being launched and it would be eight years until the iPhone appeared for the first time. It's not difficult to see how it would have been easy for a board to dismiss a robotic dog as a crazy initiative. But Sony's board didn't. AIBO was an experiment to test consumer reactions to home robots and the feasibility and reliability of this type of robot. It provided a huge source of learning for Sony's board about the potential for home robots to fulfill a wide range of purposes, including domestic work, companion roles, and medical reporting for the growing numbers of elderly people.

As well as helping the board improve its strategic sensitivity and conceive options for the firm's strategic direction, experiments also provide a lever for the board to discuss the evolution of the company with the executive. And as we discuss in chapter 7, this could be a starting point to assess the quality of the firm's strategic process.

Strategic Sensitivity: Questioning Your Thinking

While the heightened strategic sensitivity critical for the board to develop a robust strategic direction is obviously greatly dependent on external knowledge about the emerging trends that we have looked at so far, it has to be complemented by activities that further enhance strategic sensitivity by questioning the assumptions and thinking of board members. Without the challenge of different perspectives, there is a real risk that the new knowledge and insights gained through foresight, anticipation, technology scanning, listening to customers, leading indicators, and learning experiments will be interpreted and framed by the dominant logic of the firm, its existing business model, and its planned trajectory. Avoiding this danger calls for the practices of distancing, challenging, and reframing.

Distancing

In essence, distancing is about being able to step outside a company's core business and gain new and different perspectives on its potential future. It's about creating the opportunity to model the firm and its relationships to its context and consider how they might be different.

This requires actively pursuing varying viewpoints. Some of the tools and methods we have already outlined will naturally mean seeking the advice and input of external experts—for instance, in Delphi surveys or technology scanning. Broadening this concept and being aware that a diversity of perspectives is essential will serve a board well in heightening its strategic sensitivity.

Advisory boards, for instance, composed of people with different backgrounds and areas of expertise can be convened to work on specific issues related to the strategic direction. The interaction with these external experts will enrich the cognitive framing of any problem. In our own professional world, we always find the most revealing and thought-provoking gatherings are those with the greatest diversity bringing together ranks of executives, managers, financiers, policy makers, staff from nongovernmental organizations, engineers, and academics all sharing ideas and insights and finding connections between them.

Not all valuable perspectives come from outside the firm, though. Don't forget to mine the rich seam of knowledge, observations, and ideas from the company's own people. Many companies have pockets of people working on future-oriented technologies or interested in environmental issues or the impact of geopolitical events, for example, and these staff are likely to see the world, potential opportunities, and emerging inflection points very differently. Tapping into the ideas and insights of these people can be done in a variety of different ways through large-scale formal events like IBM's global "innovation jams," ongoing forums, communities of practice, and social media–based probing.

Challenging

An important part of strategic sensitivity is concerned with identifying and overcoming vulnerabilities. And to this end, small independent "red teams," tasked with challenging assumptions, decisions, commitments, and strategies, can be an invaluable tool for helping the board in essence stress test the logic and strength of its strategic direction in the context of external trends and the firm's reality (its business model, culture, processes, systems, markets, and technologies).

Originating in the military but adopted and popularized by Jack Welch at GE, the role of red teams is essentially to adopt an adversarial position and play devil's advocate against groupthink. In the context of supporting the board to develop a longer-term strategy, a red team would highlight possible ways in which competitors, customers, suppliers, or market changes could damage and even destroy the business. Those points of vulnerability then become powerful building blocks for thinking about the future.

Reframing

Reframing, or the ability to imagine new business models, is necessary for the board's work in developing the strategic direction of the company. It involves recognizing generalizable features of the firm's current business model, acknowledging its original context, and at the same time, conceptually defining which elements of this business model can be adapted to different contexts. In essence, it involves determining which parts of the current business model can be migrated over time in line with the strategic direction, and which remain dependent on the current context.

Reframing challenges the board's thinking by appraising whether there is a realistic path from the firm's current strategy to the longer-term strategic direction. If there are no points of commonality between the current business model and the long-term direction, the likelihood of renewal and transformation is pretty remote at best. So, in reframing, the board should be looking for those elements of the business model that would be foundational in the new context of the strategic direction.

■

Developing and using strong strategic sensitivity capabilities empowers the board to act as a provocative thought leader in defining a new strategic direction. And it allows the board to provide guidance and set boundaries in discussions with the CEO about the firm's near-term strategy. Having greater clarity about the future also gives a sense of purpose to staff within the company. And by defining where the company should aim to be in the next 10 years and beyond, a board is genuinely fulfilling its responsibilities to all stakeholders by identifying growth opportunities and strategic threats while also sending a clear message to analysts and investors that the company prioritizes long-term sustainability over the short-term illusion of growth.

7 ■ Understanding the Quality of the Strategy Process

Overcoming the growth curse and setting a company on the path to stronger corporate strategy isn't just about embracing an understanding of the outside world, as we discussed in chapter 6. It also necessitates a deep awareness of the strategic health of the firm. The problem is, if management is hiding the real truth about the company's health behind a smokescreen of respectable earnings, where can the board turn to get a true gauge of its strength or fragility? How can directors assess whether the nascent problems are cyclical or structural? And are there early-warning signs that, if caught and acted on, can turn the company's fortunes around before it's too late?

Putting the quality of the strategy process under the microscope will provide answers to these questions. And the long lead time from the early signs of a breakdown in the strategy process to a strategy crisis provides a reasonable window of opportunity to refocus a company that has underlying health issues but no outwardly apparent symptoms yet.

If we were to pose a question asking what Nokia, IBM, Polaroid, and ABB have in common, the fact that all four companies were victims of financial crises would be an obvious and correct observation. Yet, only five years before the high-profile demise of its mobile phone business in 2013, Nokia posted its strongest results ever, and it continued to outperform its competitors until 2010. While IBM's profits hit a high in 1989, only two years later the firm suffered massive losses and found itself struggling to survive. How could the fates of these companies appear to change so dramatically and so quickly? The answer is, they didn't. These companies had been in the throes of a strategic crisis long before their financial woes became apparent—all had been in a slow decline for a very long time.

Strategic crises, such as making wrong strategic or organizational decisions or procrastinating and freezing in the face of uncertainty, precede financial crises—often by 5 to 10 years. Yet it is rare to find managers, executives, or directors equipped to recognize the signs of a looming strategy crisis that could lead to their firm's financial demise. Leaders seem far more focused on strategy as an outcome than the quality of the strategy process.[1] And by the time they are aware of a serious problem, the damage has already been done—resources wasted, opportunities lost, morale undermined, and recovery difficult at best.

Polaroid provides a stark example of the consequences of failing to spot the signs of a strategy crisis early enough. Back in the 1980s, rifts began to emerge within Polaroid, as executives in the dominant high-margin film business refused to acknowledge the strategic opportunity of digital, which was being pursued by the electronic imaging division. Over time, tensions grew internally, and even when it became clear that digital technology was going to transform the industry, executives in the core business had become so insular in their thinking that film remained central to their "digital" strategy. Because of this, they failed to build any partnerships that were critical in the new digital ecosystem. In October 2001, Polaroid filed for bankruptcy—the result of a long-brewing, unchecked strategy crisis.

Often the small cracks that are visible to customers and to employees lower down in the company reveal faults with a firm's strategy, but they are papered over (sometimes deliberately, sometimes inadvertently), giving senior managers and directors a rosy picture of the state of a company. Some time back, while doing research at a major auto company, we were offered a loan car from the senior manager pool of new, top-of-the-range, immaculate vehicles. For the executives who made strategic decisions, their experience of the company's products was based solely on these cars. But this was a far cry from the poor reliability and durability problems customers faced as their vehicles aged and the prohibitive maintenance costs they were saddled with. We later discovered that in tough resource allocation discussions, longer-term quality issues had been bumped to the lowest priority in favor of focusing on short-term gains such as reducing manufacturing costs. The bad news about the long-term performance of the cars had not percolated up to management, and the executive car pool left managers blissfully unaware of the growing problems with the company's range.

Similarly, we are all aware of the logic of Potemkin villages in retailing, when visits by executives and directors prompt stores to be spruced up and overstaffed to give the illusion that all is well. In the years leading up to the 2017 bankruptcy of Toys "R" Us, successive rounds of spending cuts had seen cleaning crews cut to the bone, maintenance reduced at the firm's stores, and long-serving knowledgeable staff replaced with cheaper workers. At a time when the management of Toys "R" Us had painted themselves into a corner by sticking with their brick-and-mortar strategy, the unappealing state of their stores was driving customers away toward large retail groups like Walmart and Target and internet retailers. Many store managers could see the early signs of crisis, but fearful for their own livelihoods, they did their best to hide the reality on the ground from headquarters until it was too late and the group was in financial crisis.

As long as those lagging financial results and performance indicators point to a firm being in good health, why would directors go looking for trouble? It takes a great deal of bravery to put the strategy process and strategic decision-making under the spotlight. But if the board is serious about its mandate to protect the firm and the long-term interests of all stakeholders, bravery is precisely what is needed to avoid misinterpreting the early signs of decline, which will ultimately lead to a strategic crisis and the company falling victim to the growth curse.

As we have already said, a strategy crisis doesn't appear out of nowhere. It evolves from the gradual breakdown in the strategy process, which leads to a collapse in strategic thinking and poor strategic decisions. We are fortunate in having studied Nokia in depth, because the story of Nokia's mobile phone business illustrates this evolution all too vividly.[2] Although many commentators have attributed Nokia's rapid demise in mobile phones to the entry of Apple and the iPhone into the mobile communications market, Nokia was in fact collapsing strategically

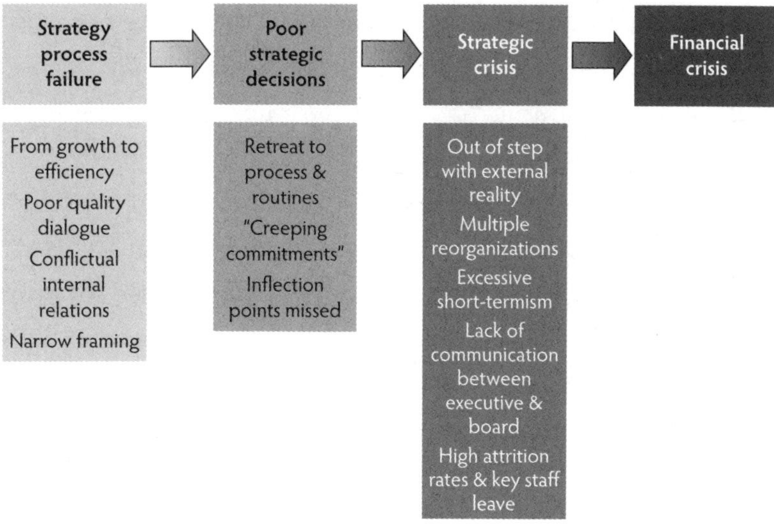

Figure 7.1: The Evolution of Strategy Failure

and organizationally long before. As we will see, the breakdown in Nokia's strategy process began more than a decade before its financial troubles surfaced. Indeed, Nokia exhibited all the telltale signs, outlined in figure 7.1, that something was wrong.

A Failure of the Strategy Process

Looking Out or Looking In?

Over time, companies become imprisoned by their own success. The external focus to find new opportunities, new markets, new customers, new partners, and new suppliers, which spurred early growth, gradually withers as companies mature, growth begins to slow, and managers turn their attention to internal, operational issues that will drive the greater efficiency needed to keep bottom-line growth respectable—in other words, the growth curse takes hold. Needless to say, seeking out efficiencies per se is not the enemy of the strategy process, but there is a danger that operational issues will take precedence, become all-consuming, and divert the attention of senior managers from engaging fully in matters relating to strategy.

And nowhere is this more apparent than at the top of companies. At a conference for nonexecutive directors at INSEAD business school, we heard plenty of anecdotal evidence confirming that when times appear to be good, far too many CEOs spend the bulk of their time and energies in their comfort zones dealing with internal and operational issues. This focus on immediate and short-term problems poses much less of a personal risk than dealing with strategic issues and the vagaries of the competitive landscape. CEOs are able to react to problems as they arise and are brought to their attention, which allows them to make quick wins that shore up their power and control.

For companies with market leadership, a certain degree of hubris also creeps in, which results in managers believing that "more of the same" (albeit bigger and incrementally better) is the right strategy to follow. Sadly, an internal, operational orientation means that once adopted, this assumption is rarely challenged, so disruptions and external challenges to the company's current strategy are much more likely to be missed. As Nokia was the global market leader for mobile phones, its senior managers, for instance, were so focused on reducing the cost of producing phones and selling more units in order to maintain their market share dominance that they dismissed the early industry rumblings around a shift to "platforms." Had they been looking outside instead of looking in, their fortunes may have been very different.

Another example of hubris blinding the strategy process is the Wall Street titan Goldman Sachs. Regulatory changes after the 2008 financial crisis (requiring increased capital holdings) made investment banking more difficult and less profitable. But unlike their main competitors who successfully diversified into new areas such as wealth and asset management, Goldman Sachs continued down the route of being the world's best pure-play investment bank. With few new geographic growth markets to conquer and profitability up and down in its core business, in 2016, Goldman Sachs opened a consumer bank, Marcus. But this move proved too little too late, and the once lauded and highly opaque company (which had an investor day for the first time in 2020) now finds itself having to face increasingly unhappy investors.

Over time, an internal focus isolates senior managers because they no longer talk to customers, suppliers, or potential partners about how their industry or the world is changing. And when that change is rapid and taking place in a complex environment, the pursuit of efficiency can be the death knell for companies as they are left without the slack needed for resilience. When everything has been cut to the bone, including morale, companies find themselves in a very fragile position, lacking the resources and energy needed to refocus or rebuild while riding out the storm.

Just when strategy needs to be agile and innovative to avoid the growth curse, the myopic, internal focus of the CEO and senior executives unleashes a cycle that leads to irreversible decline. The more the company falls behind market or industry changes, the more an internal focus is reinforced to maintain bottom-line growth. Without any genuine strategic growth options, executives make every effort to keep shareholders happy by boosting short-term results. For instance, while IBM's integrated business model was struggling against new technologies and new competitors in the mid-2000s, CEO Sam Palmisano announced a plan to double earnings per share over a five-year period—a pledge that he later renewed for a further five years. Achieving these short-term results meant cutting spending on the very resources (strategic assets) that are needed to reignite growth, such as research and development (R&D), marketing, and creative staff, and axing investment in new businesses—leaving IBM highly vulnerable.

Luckily for the board, the indicators that point to the early-warning signs of a shift from a healthy external focus to a harmful internal one are easy and straightforward to spot. And a simple annual audit along strategic, organizational, and behavioral aspects, as outlined in figure 7.2, will highlight problem areas that, if caught early enough, can be reversed.[3] The figure can also serve as a handy checklist for externally focused

Indicators		**Internal** Focus	**External** Focus
Strategic			
	Objectives	Efficiency	Growth, innovation
	Management	By input	By output
	Metrics	ROE	ROI
	Fund allocation	Dividends, buybacks	Investments
Organizational			
	Power structure	Hierarchical, centralized	Decentralized, networked
	Resource allocation	Budgets	Projects
	Top team	"Yes" men	Differentiated contributors
	Communication	Secretive, silos	Open, participative
Behavioral			
	Top team process	One-to-one	Open, inclusive
	Time & attention	Inside the firm	Outside the firm
	Individual priority	Personal interest	Good citizenship

Figure 7.2: Are You Internally or Externally Oriented? Developed from original by Andrea Cuomo.

executives to help prevent them from turning to the slippery slope of looking inward.

Dialogue or Monologue?

Open and honest discussion and dialogue between managers, the executive team, the CEO, and the board about the future direction of the company, the industry, the potential threats both face, and general sense-making of what is happening in and around the company is a sign of a healthy strategy process. When this doesn't happen and the CEO and executive team are aloof and isolated, a growing reluctance and fear to even acknowledge the potential need for alternative strategic paths can permeate a company.

Fueling the growth curse, a lack of dialogue points to a culture in which uncomfortable truths are not acknowledged, and in a negative feedback loop, this leads to more unrealistic expectations and further inevitable failure. This was the case at Ford before Alan Mulally took over in 2006. Ford had long operated as a series of fiefdoms in which executives never cooperated and made decisions based on the best outcome for their own career, their division, and the company, in that order. In executive meetings, unrealistic optimism prevailed, and bad news was always buried. In fact, dialogue was nonexistent, and executive meetings were peppered with barbed comments and jokes made at other people's expense. One of Mulally's first priorities on joining Ford was to bring about open, honest dialogue, and to do this, he had to make his executive team feel secure. When the first executive admitted to having a problem in his division at the weekly executive team meeting, Mulally went out of his way to praise him for being "visible." Gradually, the permafrost began to melt; more executives opened up and realized that open dialogue in fact led to real cooperation and finding solutions for what had seemed unsurmountable problems.

Ed Catmull's lessons from his leadership of Pixar over the years shows the importance of openness and, in particular, the ongoing quest for candor (as opposed to honesty, with its moral connotations) in conversations of strategic importance.[4]

During the making of *Toy Story 2*, a small informal group made up of people who had worked on the original film was formed to try and improve the sequel. Nicknamed "the Braintrust," this group grew to include a wider range of people in the company, from producers to creatives. Their role was to provide advice and constructive criticism periodically throughout the making of a new movie and to protect directors against project myopia.

In his book *Creativity, Inc.*, Catmull describes the hallmarks of Braintrust meetings as being "frank talk, spirited debate, laughter and love." He explains that "a lively debate in a Braintrust meeting is not being waged in the hopes of any one person winning the day" but to tease out the truth, no matter how uncomfortable that may be. And to ensure people felt safe to speak with candor at Braintrust meetings, as president of Pixar, Catmull tried to attend all meetings, noting, "The fear of saying something stupid and looking bad, of offending someone or being intimidated, of retaliating or being retaliated against—they all have a way of reasserting themselves. And when they do, you must address them squarely." Interestingly, Steve Jobs (who at the time was CEO of Pixar) was not involved in Braintrust meetings because it was agreed that with his often abrasive style and dominant personality, he would have been an impediment to the valuable open dialogues and discussions.

It's not just bad organizational cultures that are the enemy of quality strategy dialogues—language can play a role, too. Even if directors, the CEO, and the executive team all have strong strategic minds, their ability to be collectively strategic can be stymied if the language they use to discuss strategy weakens the quality of their interactions. And by "language," we mean the level of abstractness at which matters are discussed (as opposed to non-native speakers misinterpreting specific nuances, for example). In research a few years ago, we found that for strategic discourse to be effective, an intermediate level of language is needed. When the language used is mired in too much detail, it risks missing the big picture—not seeing the forest for the trees. At the other extreme, language that is at too high a level of abstraction makes it difficult to translate ideas and concepts into action points.[5]

We have all been in meetings and found ourselves perplexed by language that seems designed to confuse and confound— strings of buzzwords and acronyms seemingly threaded together to defy interpretation. But the language of strategy dialogues should be plain and clear—a constructive tool, not a defensive weapon. Just as entrepreneurs are encouraged to explain their business proposition in a concise elevator pitch, so too should the outcomes of strategy dialogues be easily summarized in a straightforward and succinct manner. It is simple enough for the board to ask the CEO and executive team to provide concise summaries of their strategy dialogues. If they are unable to do so collectively, they probably aren't using clear language.

Assessing the quality of the strategic dialogue in your company isn't straightforward, but figure 7.3 outlines some of the differences between a high-quality strategic dialogue and a poor one. And plotting where you are on each of these measures will

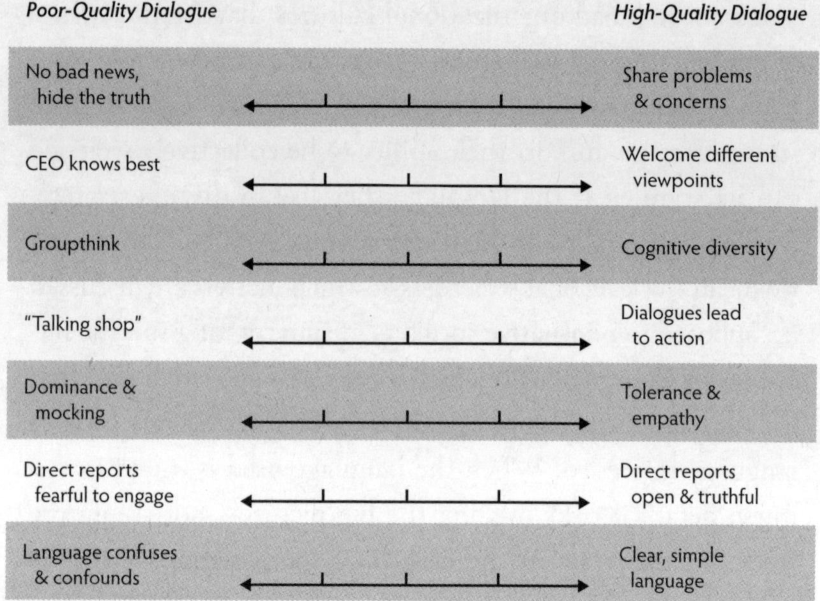

Figure 7.3: How Strong Is the Quality of Your Strategy Dialogue?

give an indication of how robust the dialogue element of your strategy process is.

Harmony or Conflict?

Without an open and honest dialogue, the strategy process will weaken further as internal factions and vested interests strengthen. In multibusiness companies lacking corporate coherence or a shared strategic agenda, individual business units will coalesce around their own interests and shut themselves off from other businesses within the company. This is more likely to happen when the relationship between the CEO and senior executives is based on one-to-one discussions and not conducted as a mutually dependent team. Personal rivalries between individual executives can be quick to develop and will deepen as factions form around these individuals, eventually pitting business unit against business unit. The whole culture becomes combative.

Returning to the case of Nokia, by the early 2000s the core mobile phone business was so stretched by a combination of its success, market dominance, and ever-increasing short-term performance pressures that the innovation mantle had informally been taken up by the relatively small Tampere development center (a legacy from Nokia's earlier computer-related activities). This R&D hub had recognized early on the potential of data communications and was responsible for the launch of the world's first smartphone, the Nokia Communicator, in 1996 and Nokia's first camera phone in 2001. Yet rather than embrace the ideas and skills of this unit, executives in the core phone business saw Tampere's data activities as a threat. A dysfunctional internal rivalry developed that effectively cut the visionary Tampere unit out of the strategic conversation, ultimately to the detriment of Nokia's ability to compete in a changing environment.

Incentives also play a big part here. When the executive team's incentives are skewed toward the results of their own business unit, most executives will naturally prioritize achieving strong results in their unit over contributing to the broader corporate strategy process. Strategy dialogues fall victim to dysfunction and intransigence, with each faction arguing their point but rarely conceding ground to others.

When relationships between businesses and between individuals are conflictual, most people will feel the tension—but in this type of atmosphere, few will be prepared to speak out. So how can boards assess how harmonious (or not) relations are in the company that they oversee? Fortunately, there are proxies that can indicate the extent to which factions have emerged. A simple audit of cross-team or business unit collaboration or joint projects can speak volumes. Surveys administered by third parties can reveal the extent to which the executive team are collectively committed to the strategy process and can unearth underlying tensions. And structured network analysis will give a picture of who is talking to whom about what.

Broad or Narrow Framing?

Left unchecked, companies built around a dominant, successful core business can find this becomes detrimental to the quality of the strategy process because confirmation bias sets in, so potential new opportunities are framed through the narrow lens of what appears to be a successful current strategy. In Nokia's case, this resulted in an early failure to embrace "data" in the core mobile phone business; in IBM's case, the mainframe business was continued long after it was clear that it would be eroded by the arrival of personal computers; and at both Polaroid and Kodak, narrow framing put the preservation of their high-margin film business at the core of new digital strategies—a lack of fit that was doomed to failure. To avoid the dangers of narrow framing (or tunnel vision) calls for a more open or "fuzzy" business definition and vision that leaves room for alternative business models. (It is worth noting that when a board defines and shares the strategic direction of the firm, it will provide a broader context to help avoid the pitfalls of narrow framing.)

Fledgling business models that are crucial to the strategic renewal essential for avoiding the growth curse rely on experimentation and are usually protected and nurtured in a ventures-type program. However, when the strategy process begins to break down, there is a real danger that the assessment of these new ventures is contaminated and also falls victim to narrow framing.

They are likely to be vetted in light of how they contribute to the dominant business rather than the potential new opportunities they represent. And they will often be subject to unrealistic targets and metrics, ensuring none will have the opportunity to grow and risk cannibalizing the core business.

To guard against this, the board, together with the CEO and executive team, can assess the company's current portfolio of new businesses or experiments against the strategic direction of the firm. If the two are a complete mismatch, then serious questions need to be asked about how the company will achieve its longer-term ambition if none of its strategic bets are pointing the company in that direction.

Poor Strategic Decisions

The obvious result of a failing strategy process is that poor strategic decisions are made that severely compromise a company's ability to avoid the growth curse because continuity is favored over renewal. A breakdown in the strategy process often leaves beleaguered senior executives retreating to their comfort zones and hiding behind procedures and routines rather than standing up to the CEO and their peers, voicing alternative views, being challenged, and potentially being found wanting. It becomes normal for the CEO and executive team to seek out and interpret information that supports the company's entrenched orthodoxies and their own preconceptions. They become focused on managing their reputation and self-interest rather than the business and its growth potential. This leads to an asymmetric view of risk and reward, where the risk from change is perceived as much greater and potentially more damaging than the reward from continuing down the same track (whereas in reality, the greater risk is from strategic stagnation and long-term decline). And so the quality of strategic decisions slips into a self-reinforcing downward spiral.

With the collapse of a strategy process, strategic decisions are more likely to be influenced by excessive path dependence or "creeping commitments" stemming from fragmented decisions of the past. Even if these earlier decisions no longer make sense for future strategy, without a robust process to challenge them, firms are locked into these commitments financially and organizationally, and often managers are psychologically bound by them, too. The Symbian operating system was just such a creeping commitment for Nokia. It had initially been adopted as an effective solution for the second-generation Communicator and gave Nokia an early competitive advantage. Over time, Nokia became committed to Symbian across its growing range of phones, even though it was an unwieldy, product-centric operating system that required new coding for each phone model. By the time it became obvious that the commitment to Symbian was detrimental to Nokia's strategic options in what had become a platform- and application-centric world, Nokia was trapped. Symbian had become too big and integrated to allow Nokia to easily switch to an alternative operating system.

Inflection points are much more likely to be missed as conservatism settles in and as the company's senior executives and managers shift their attention away from the strategy process and toward classic growth curse behavior of shoring up the current business. It is easy to dismiss the early signals of a major change in the industry, technology, or market, particularly if your business has enjoyed market leadership for a number of years. Existing business models tend to be resilient to change—the risk of value migration is very real (and to be avoided); it is difficult to rebuild or replicate embedded competencies and ecosystems; and strong vested interests (from governments, suppliers, customers, and partners) can coalesce around an entrenched business model.

Most successful and mature companies will also be victims of inertia in the face of an inflection point, simply because people inside the company just can't imagine that things could change so radically and the company's dominance could be toppled. When inflection points are missed, the perceived need to play catch-up usually results in yet more bad strategic decisions—made too hastily and without either looking beyond the current inflection point or thinking about the systemic impact on the company's current strategy or structures.

The Strategy Crisis

By the time a company reaches a strategic crisis, the accumulated outcomes of the breakdown in the strategy process and a slew of poor strategic decisions will be all too apparent. It will be clear internally that the company is out of step with the reality of its industry, even though the outside world may not yet be aware of this. While Apple and then Google were beginning to redefine the industry around mobile communications and competing on platforms and applications, Nokia was still micro-segmenting the market in a bid to sell more hardware (phones) to more people. And in a crowded digital camera market in which ecosystems played a vital part in supplying specialized components at low costs, Kodak embarked on developing and manufacturing its digital cameras entirely in-house.

Another sure sign that a strategy crisis is underway is when CEOs seem to be continually rearranging the proverbial deck chairs as the Titanic sinks. Or, to put it more plainly, they undertake unnecessary (and disruptive) reorganizations believing new structures, rather than a new strategy, will provide a panacea to the company's problems. ABB, for example, undertook three major reorganizations in the eight years leading up to its financial crisis in 2001. Between 2004 and Nokia's near bankruptcy in 2013, executives had restructured the firm four times.

In a more recent example, strategy failure may have been halted by investor intervention at Danone, the French multinational food company. In October 2020, CEO Emmanuel Faber announced the company's fifth reorganization in seven years—an indication that all was not well, despite Danone looking, on the surface, like a model of stakeholder capitalism. With the support of the founding family, Faber had championed environmental activism, and in 2020, shareholders overwhelmingly supported Danone changing its legal status to an "entreprise à mission"—a company with a social purpose as well as a shareholder one. But these lofty ambitions masked a failing strategy: Danone had overpaid for acquisitions, demographic changes meant key segments such as baby food were naturally shrinking, and Faber's stated strategy of becoming an environmentally friendly, higher-margin company lacked a detailed "how to." Under pressure from shareholders, who found Danone's strategy unconvincing and the prospect of yet another reorganization frustrating, Faber was fired by the board in March 2021. The fact that it was shareholders who highlighted the company's failing strategy reflects badly on the board and illustrates the necessity for a more strategic form of governance if boards are to genuinely fulfill their role in ensuring the long-term prosperity of the firms they oversee.

When a company has reached a strategy crisis, the relationship between the executive and board will also be in crisis, with members of the executive team rarely and only reluctantly communicating with the board. With the CEO being left as the primary conduit of information to the board, it is unlikely directors will get a real sense of quite how perilous the company's strategic position is.

Senior executives and managers who are in the know begin to leave the firm, and even those that remain may well sell their shares in an attempt to get out before the inevitable financial crisis hits. Outside the executive ranks, staff will feel all too keenly the lack of investment in growth and innovation and the endless cuts in training, expenses, or even the maintenance of facilities. Combined with the relentless pressure to meet unfeasible targets, morale plummets and staff who were once loyal leave to pursue opportunities elsewhere.

Answers to the following simple questions can reveal whether the strategy process has collapsed and you are in the midst of a strategy crisis:

> Does your company seem to be out of step with innovation in the industry?
>
> Have you undertaken more than one major reorganization in the last four years?
>
> Do the board and executive team interact regularly, and are these interactions open, honest, and informative?
>
> Have attrition rates throughout the firm increased in the last few years, and are they in line with the industry average?

■

Turning things around once you have reached a strategy crisis is rare and extremely difficult. But when a board monitors the strategy process and is alert to the early signs of decay, directors can take action to reposition the company for renewal. It won't be easy. It will take courage and vision to arrest the decay at a time when financial performance indicators erroneously point to all being well. However, confronting this unavoidable challenge is crucial to avoid the continued pursuit of short-term quarterly growth gains from a maturing business while waiting for an inevitable financial collapse.

8 ■ Getting the CEO and Executive Team Right

We began this book by examining the growth curse and the role CEOs play in perpetuating the illusion of growth and, in so doing, hastening the demise of the firms they lead. Having then gone on to look at the roles and responsibilities the board needs to undertake to arrest short-termism and support the long-term prosperity of the firm for the benefit of all stakeholders, we now return to the subject of the CEO. More precisely, what attributes, skills, and experience should the board look for (and avoid) in a CEO?

Breaking the growth curse cycle and having a greater focus on meeting sustainable stakeholder needs calls for collective leadership and responsibility. That's not to say the importance of the role of the CEO is in any way diminished, merely the emphasis has to change, as good strategy emerges from the process of interaction between the CEO and the board. There is no room for heroic leadership or power-hungry narcissism. Instead, good CEOs enable, motivate, and energize the executive team and wider organization. They orchestrate essential leadership unity so that they can work with the board and other executives on fine-tuning and implementing strategy. They set the tone for the behavior and culture toward colleagues, subordinates, suppliers, customers, partners, and shareholders.

When boards have defined a robust long-term strategic direction for the company as we described in chapter 6, and have a good understanding of the quality of the strategy process as outlined in the previous chapter, they will be much better equipped to consider the following question: Do we have the right CEO in place?

Do You Have the Right CEO?

Once the board has defined a clear ambition for the firm, there may be circumstances where the incumbent CEO may choose to step down or the board may wish to make a leadership change. The CEO may simply lack the necessary skill set to develop and deliver new strategic options. CEOs who have been in the role for some time may lack the energy and drive needed to lead the firm in a new direction. One board chair we spoke with explained that in mature businesses, it is unrealistic to expect long-serving CEOs to spearhead redirections or transformation, as this would require them to question everything they have already done and then mobilize the company, investors, and partners around a new strategy.

As we touched on in chapter 3, there are many instances in which incumbent CEOs need to be replaced because they have become an intractable part of the problem. For instance, CEOs who are overly focused on meeting quarterly forecasts and short-term results are more likely to misrepresent information they feed to the board and may instill a culture of fear and infighting throughout all levels in the firm. This is not a foundation on which long-term sustainable renewal can be built. Alternatively, recall the progression from a breakdown in the strategy process to a financial crisis, as discussed in chapter 7. An incumbent may still be riding high if the visible signs of a strategy crisis (though known internally) are not yet evident to the outside world. In this case, the CEO, to maintain control and power, may have lost self-awareness and could slowly but surely drive the company into the ground.

Throw narcissism into the mix, and the problems increase. The superiority felt by narcissists leads them to believe their own decisions will naturally produce the best results.[1] Consequently, they don't like to have their own point of view challenged by either a board of directors or members of an executive team. Narcissists put considerable effort into building a strong, positive public image and will not shrink from reminding directors of their rare and valuable talents while also turning on considerable charm in order to get their way with boards. When a narcissist CEO is also the chair of the board, the problem of control is exacerbated.

Narcissist CEOs tend to select members of the executive team and other senior managers who won't stand up to or disagree with them, and if these executives do, they tend to find themselves subjugated by various forms of bullying. With lower levels of empathy and intimacy, narcissists will readily exploit and dominate those they work with because they don't value the efforts and contributions of others.[2] But they are equally happy to take all the credit for successful outcomes instigated by other executives.[3] In other words, they are definitely not team players and thus are incapable of the deeply collaborative effort required to bring about a change in strategy and the fortunes of the company.

Or Do You Have a Plan to Change the CEO?

A further problem with narcissist CEOs arises when it comes to succession planning. Their fragile egos mean they are less likely to have mentored and nurtured a bench of potential successors. And so, should the incumbent CEO need replacing because of illness, sudden dismissal, or resignation, the board is left in the awkward position of having to find a new CEO without having any insight about the strengths of internal candidates. Narcissist CEOs will have ensured they are the only ones who communicate with the board.

But more generally, unplanned successions create wider immediate problems. They tend to leave the board finding themselves stepping into the breach and being drawn into more immediate strategy-related decision-making. And for most boards, this comes as a shock with a steep learning curve as they suddenly have to grapple with a Pandora's box of stalling growth, failing strategy, weak strategic assets, low morale, and no apparent or obvious strategic options.

Unfortunately, this is not as uncommon as one would expect. HP, for instance, experienced two unplanned successions in a row. In 2005, HP's board fired Carly Fiorina after she served five years as CEO, with no successor in place. Fast-forward to

2010, and HP's board fired its next CEO Mark Hurd, again with no plans for succession. But failing to have a strategic grasp of the company and its situation, the board plowed ahead with Hurd's strategy and, in the three months after Hurd's departure, spent almost $9 billion on acquisitions and share buybacks—at a time that the company had been cut to the bone and its cash reserves were very low. The failure of HP's board to set a strategic direction and its lack of understanding of the state of the company's strategy process contributed to it hiring Leo Apotheker as the next CEO. Apotheker rapidly began implementing his own strategic vision, and when shareholders started objecting, the board infamously fired him after less than a year in the role.[4]

In November 2022, on the back of an unpopular reorganization, a number of public relations blunders, an increasingly autocratic management style, and poor earnings, Disney's board fired Bob Chapek after he had only been in the CEO role for less than two years. With no credible succession plan in place, the board of Disney brought back Bob Iger, the former CEO and Chapek's predecessor. Although having already served 15 years at the helm of Disney, Iger has reportedly only agreed to stay in the role for two years, which should give the board time to find a suitable replacement.[5]

If the CEO, executive team, and board work together undertaking the various strategy assessments that we propose in the following chapters, in a climate of reciprocal respect and collaboration, it follows that there should be less likelihood of an unplanned succession leaving the company in turmoil. Both the long-term direction and medium-term strategy that fit the capabilities of the company will be clear and agreed. And from working with the executive team on the various iterative strategy assessments, the board will have a good understanding of strengths and shortcomings of each potential internal CEO candidate.

But succession planning should not stop at the topmost layer of executives. Talent needs to be spotted and nurtured further down the firm, too, so you don't lose your future executive team to your competitors or exciting new start-ups. Surveys from the likes of Boston Consulting Group and PwC show that firms have significant gaps in their pipelines to fill senior management roles. And demographics can explain why: There are now fewer people in the 35 to 44 age group—the pool for up-and-coming executives—than in the retiring baby-boomer generation.[6] And to make talent management more difficult, individuals in this age group are less likely to stay with large companies and more likely than previous generations of managers to join start-ups or exciting high-growth new firms.

Good CEOs working with good boards know how vital a transparent and honest succession planning process is. Looking again at HP, when Lewis Platt stepped down as CEO, there were a handful of strong internal candidates to take over. But without any warning or explanation, the board hired Carly Fiorina, a nonengineer from outside the company with neither CEO experience nor a background in any of HP's businesses. Not surprisingly, given how the board had handled this situation, many of the senior executives at HP who were in line for the role were unhappy with the board's decision, and this ill feeling deepened when it became obvious that neither the board nor Fiorina had a clear strategy for HP. The actions of HP's board were unfair to both the internal candidates who were overlooked and to the new CEO they hired.

In the climate they created, critical leadership unity would prove very difficult to build.

Minimizing Mistakes and "Casting" Errors

When a board's involvement in strategy is limited to signing off on plans the CEO brings to them, it is easy to see how the CEO succession or hiring process itself can become dysfunctional and fall victim to the growth curse. Facing an unholy trinity of stalling growth, growing shareholder pressure, and a very limited grasp of the company's strategy, ambition, or strategic options, boards often fail to seek a candidate with the skills and drive to overcome these challenges. Instead the board turns to high-profile external CEOs whose star qualities they hope will dazzle analysts, the media, and shareholders.[7] Our discussions with a number of executive search specialists confirmed that when boards approach them with a CEO search, quite often those boards are unable to specify what they need in the new CEO. They may have come up with a generic list of meaningless attributes—a composite of "great leader traits"— and so it falls to the search firm to try and tease out the critical skills and qualities the candidates should meet.

Once a list of potential candidates has been whittled down, few directors have the skills to properly evaluate them, and most would struggle to map candidate competencies to the requirements of their firm. Studies by executive search firm Egon Zehnder found that less than 30 percent of board directors had knowledge of assessment methods, and the majority had no experience or had been involved in just one CEO succession before.[8] When a board is trying to hire a celebrity CEO, more often than not, instead of interviewing the candidate for suitability, directors spend their time "courting" the candidate, selling the company and role to them instead of the other way around. Thus, critical questions go unasked.

Without either a clear understanding of the qualities needed in a new CEO or the tools and skills to assess candidates with some degree of accuracy, boards risk being swayed by confident, charismatic, extrovert candidates, even though they may not be the best choice for the role. In fact, highly confident candidates are twice as likely to be offered a CEO role even though once in situ, they are less likely to meet the expectations of the board and shareholders.[9]

Given that many boards take this rather amateur approach to finding a new CEO, the number of CEO failures is hardly surprising. However, when boards are involved in the strategy process, they will understand what is called for from a new CEO and, with the help of a search firm, be able to articulate the experience and skills needed to meet the company's strategic requirements.

The Right CEO for the Structure

When considering CEO candidates, the structure of the company also has a bearing on suitability. For instance, in a pure-play company, the CEO will need to work with the executive team to develop and implement one strategy. Whereas in a multibusiness firm, the situation differs. As we will see in chapter 9, corporate should contribute value added, so the "group" CEO will need to be someone comfortable operating at that higher level. With the individual businesses each having their own specific strategies developed and implemented by their leadership teams, the role of the group CEO is to focus on the umbrella strategy so that the contribution of each business in the portfolio is enhanced by it being part of the group. This requires someone with considerable skills, not only as a strategist able to meld multiple strategic threads into an overall strategic logic, but as an arbiter and team builder between the different businesses.

Deeply rooted self-assurance becomes even more important for CEOs in multibusiness firms, particularly if one of the business units is highly successful—in which case, the visibility of the head of that business both internally and externally may well begin to eclipse that of the group CEO.

Should the CEO Be a "Fit" or a Change Agent?

The strategic direction defined by the board (chapter 6), together with the outcomes of the board's analysis of the current state of the strategy process in the firm (chapter 7), will determine to what extent a new CEO should fit into a company's existing context and culture or be brought in to change them. This speaks directly to the issues around internal versus external candidates.

Internal candidates offer some clear advantages, especially when continuity is desirable. They understand the company's culture, processes, its products or services, its customers and suppliers. They should know the strengths (and weak points) each of their colleagues could bring to an executive team role. And as insiders, they have a "warts and all" perspective of the firm and can hit the ground running. These attributes probably explain why studies have shown that internal CEO hires generally stay with the company for longer and tend to perform better despite getting paid less than their external counterparts.[10] And of course, the management style, capabilities, and general performance of internal candidates will be well known in the company, making them much less of a gamble than an unknown external hire. These traits are clearly valued by many boards, particularly as companies navigate their way out of the disruptions caused by the COVID pandemic. In 2021, 86 percent of new CEO appointments in S&P 500 companies were internal hires while at Russell 3000 firms, the figure was 71 percent.[11]

Even so, this fuller knowledge can sometimes go against inside hires. With so much detail about an internal candidate, directors may be drawn into dwelling on small negatives in their records—things that would never come to light with an external candidate. It can also be difficult for boards to look beyond the role an internal candidate is currently in and see how to transpose their skills into the requirements of a CEO role, whereas the external candidate faces no such bias.

But what if change rather than continuity is required? Do internal candidates still measure up against their external rivals? Research has shown that one particular type of internal candidate excels in CEO roles that call for change—the "inside outsiders."[12] Having worked for the company for a long time, these people understand the culture, the process, the politics—in other words, how the company works. But they have also spent time in roles away from headquarters—perhaps working as country heads or business unit leaders or running major alliances—and this gives them an outsider's view of the company, too. They see what can and needs to change and have a vision of how to do it. So, even though these people may not be immediately visible vying for attention in a headquarters role, they should be sought out as potential candidates.

More often than not, when a clear change in strategy and/ or culture is called for, external candidates are usually sought, particularly when a company is in trouble. Although outsiders have the benefits of not being mired in the company's politics and having a different perspective, it is important to remember that these candidates will bring with them the intellectual and practice baggage from other companies where they have worked—and this can be a good or a bad thing. Let's return to the experience of 3M as an example. 3M was a company with the processes, structure, and culture to deliver a continual stream of innovations. There was plenty of slack in the system— time-wise, budget-wise, and culturally—to allow experimentation and discovery while risk taking, tolerance, collaboration, and long-termism were imbued in the culture.

As globalization intensified in the 1990s, though, 3M found fast followers moving into many of its high-margin niche markets, and sales growth slowed. An internal study revealed that on average, 3M spent as much time developing a product that resulted in sales of around $250,000 a year as it did on one that brought in revenues of $10 million a year. Clearly, some things needed to change, and in 2000, the board's response was to hire James McNerney from GE. He became 3M's first outside as well as its first nonengineer or scientist CEO.

A protégé of Jack Welch, McNerney arrived at 3M ready to implement the complete GE management toolkit. His first act as CEO was to announce ambitious stretch goals of doubling sales and operating earnings in less than 10 years. To achieve these goals, McNerney introduced Six Sigma throughout 3M's research and development and manufacturing operations. As a disciple of internal competition, he centralized resource allocation with a new corporate center to focus budgets on high-growth projects that could yield fast results. The GE playbook had no time for the high failure rates that underpinned 3M's innovation and experimentation culture, and so McNerney redirected focus to improving existing product lines (i.e., lowering costs) rather than spending time on "inventions." And he cut the firm's famous 15 percent rule, which had been in place since 1948 and enabled all staff to feed their curiosity by spending up to 15 percent of their time on their experiments and ideas. Over the years, this policy, which might have looked frivolous and lacking in focus and efficiency when viewed from the GE perspective, had actually been responsible for a wide range of successful 3M products, including Scotch tape, Post-it notes, and adhesives for transdermal drug delivery.[13] 3M's future-oriented corporate lab was split into divisions aligned with the business groups reporting to the business heads. And to keep everyone on their toes, McNerney introduced quarterly financial reporting.

Transplanting GE systems, processes, and practices to a creative, innovative, and agile company like 3M was like using a sledgehammer to crack a nut. Everything about 3M called for a leadership style that created the conditions for innovation to flourish across multiple product segments, whereas the GE leadership style was about controlling and managing businesses with a single core product. During McNerney's tenure, 3M's nonpolitical, egalitarian, low-ego, and highly collaborative culture had been crushed. Morale was at an all-time low. And Six Sigma had led to the dramatic fall in the number of new products in 3M's pipeline. It would take the lighter touch of McNerney's successor—reinstating the practices and processes that supported innovation—to resurrect 3M's culture and long-term viability.

So, in considering external candidates from companies with strong cultures and processes, boards need to ask themselves to what extent they want a new CEO to change the context and culture of the company. Do they want their company to be remade in the image of the firm the new CEO comes from? Will the likely changes they implement enhance or further damage the company's strategic options and long-term direction? And will the arrival of a new CEO with such a different approach reignite energy or risk losing key members of the executive team and senior management talent?

The Working Relationship at the Top

Having a CEO with the skills to develop and execute strategic options that align with the strategic direction of the company is obviously critical. But the CEO has an equally important role working with the board and the executive team. And so the CEO's ability to collaborate, coach, and consult should not be overlooked.

The working relationship between the CEO and board obviously has to respect certain boundaries. As illustrated in figure 8.1, while the board is responsible for setting the strategic direction of the company, the CEO has responsibility for developing and executing the near- to midterm strategy. Because there is some overlap between these roles, both parties need to understand emerging trends, and it is helpful if the CEO and board actively assess the quality of the strategy process in the firm (as described in chapter 7). Part of the board's process for setting the strategic direction will involve collaborating with the CEO to assess the firm's strategic assets, its strategic agility, and the strategic options available (discussed further in chapters 9

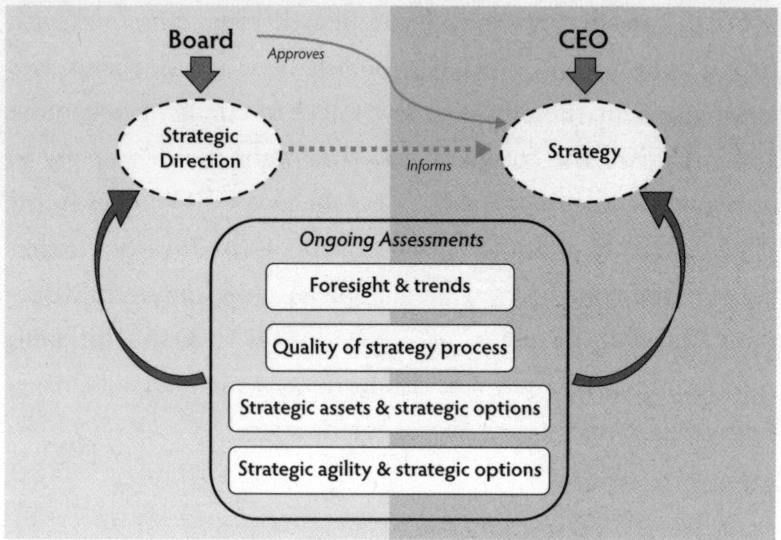

Figure 8.1: Contributions to Strategy at the Top

and 10). And the CEO's strategy has to take account of the strategic direction.

In short, the board and CEO have to work together in an iterative fashion. For the CEO's strategy to make sense, the CEO has to first understand the logic and rationale behind the board's strategic direction (and this itself will be dynamic and adjusting over time). With this in mind, the CEO can begin developing a strategy that both fits the strategic direction and addresses the more immediate challenges the company faces. An engaged board of the type we described in chapter 5 will provide the CEO with a natural strategic sparring partner or sounding board for testing ideas and seeking input and feedback. The interaction between the board and CEO over strategy is, then, an ongoing process that leads to more robust outcomes and a strong shared commitment; it is definitely not an annual exercise in which the board directors "sign off" on the strategy the CEO brings to them.

Moving on to the working relationship between the CEO and the executive team, leadership unity is key. The CEO should select an executive team not only based on their expertise and the CEO's ability to trust and work effectively with each individual, but on the dynamics between members of the team. They have to perform well in their specific roles and as a group—welcoming advice and insights from each other, reaching a consensus without acrimony, and being able to frame issues so that interdependencies are clearly understood.

The strength of a coherent executive team can be seen in what was known as Nokia's "Dream Team"—the group of executives responsible for the phenomenal rise of Nokia in the 1990s. CEO Jorma Ollila assembled a tight-knit and trusted team with very different personalities, cognitive styles, and complementary skills—a natural reflective strategist able to cope with uncertainty and ambiguity; a performance-focused, action-oriented manager drawn to solving operational problems; a rigorous and disciplined finance and operations officer who could shift effortlessly between detail and the big picture; and a talented strategist and shrewd negotiator with dogged determination. Working closely with the CEO, the Dream Team led Nokia from near bankruptcy to dominate the mobile phone industry by recognizing and using cross-company synergies, linking operational strategy, putting the interests of the Nokia group before that of their own divisions, and supporting each other to ensure things got done.

If boards are to play a more active role in safeguarding a firm's future, they also need to build relationships with the executive team and senior-most managers. These relationships are important for several reasons:

First, as we saw earlier relating to succession planning, it's vital that the board is able to directly assess the potential candidates for the CEO role, and there is no better way to do this than by actively working with them.

Second, direct relations between board members and executives guard against the CEO controlling the information flow to the board and give the board a better understanding of any issues and problems the company may be facing. It is worth noting that if a CEO opposes executives having one-on-one discussions with the board, this reflects a "controlling" tendency and signals that it is very unlikely the CEO has a good working relationship with the executive team.

Third, directors have a wealth of experience and insight as well as wide networks that executives should be able to draw on when needed. But it is important that cliques or one-on-one relationships don't develop. To keep everyone in the loop, written memos of conversations between directors and executives can be circulated to the board and CEO.

Fourth, in multibusiness firms, the board needs to work with business heads to have a good understanding of the state of each business and its preparedness for the future. While the group CEO will help ensure that the strategy of each business is aligned with the overriding corporate strategy, the iterative process of strategy making at the business level will no doubt benefit from board involvement.

Finally, the quality of the executive team and the layers of management reporting to these executives are factors in how much drive, commitment, and energy the company has in reserve to pursue a new strategic direction. The only way the board can assess these factors is through direct interaction with executives.

▪

The growth curse—or quest for short-term growth—pursued by omnipotent CEOs and left unchecked by boards has resulted in a strategy vacuum at the top of many mature companies, leaving them vulnerable and fragile. And little can be salvaged in the long term with the wrong type of leader in place and poor succession planning that fails to identify and nurture strong replacement candidates. But with the right CEO at the helm to collaborate more closely with the board in the strategy process, genuine options for renewal can be explored and the future of the company made more certain.

MAKING STRATEGY STRONGER

What are the alternatives to the search for relentless short-term growth, particularly for large mature companies at the plateau of the S-curve? It's clear that trying to keep the growth illusion alive ultimately fails. Perhaps it's time we were realistic and accepted that continued linear or exponential growth will always come to an end and the key to long-term sustainability is accepting and managing slowing growth in the core business while at the same time understanding and pursuing the strategic options for renewal. Part Three outlines the board's role in assessing those strategic options and the conditions that must be in place for renewal to be successful.

9 ■ Strategic Assets and Strategic Options

Assessing the strength (or otherwise) of a company's strategic assets should be a critical and ongoing collaborative exercise for the board, CEO, and executive management team because a shared perspective on strategic assets is an essential ingredient for the strategic dialogue within a firm.

When setting a "strategic direction," the board needs to take into account the company's strategic assets, because any imagined future has to be rooted in the reality of what is achievable, and strategic assets provide the critical building blocks needed. And in terms of the here and now, the board and executive have to be sure that the company's strategic assets support the near-term strategy (which the board signs off); that they will allow the company to be strategically agile in the face of immediate challenges and emerging inflection points; and that the company is not underleveraging or overextending its strategic assets, as either scenario has implications for the strategic options available and where investments need to be made.

Before examining the dynamics, challenges, and methods of assessing them, let us first remind ourselves what constitutes value-creating strategic assets.

Strategic Assets 101

The essence of strategic assets can be found in four defining characteristics:[1]

They are rare or, even better, unique.

They are distinctive and hard to substitute. It is difficult to compete and succeed in the firm's business without them, which makes them particularly valuable.

They are not easily imitable. The faster the attempt to imitate strategic assets, the higher the costs and risks of failure because:

- They are often embedded in collective know-how and skills that have been built up over a long time and can be difficult to observe from the outside.
- They can result from a long history of trusting relationships or a collaborative culture within the firm and with suppliers and customers.
- They are usually complementary to other strategic assets that are part of an activity system (either internal or within a wider ecosystem), and this

creates strength because the causal links and contributions of specific assets may be hard to distinguish.

They are not tradable. They do not leak easily, and they cannot be uprooted and cloned. The only way they can be sold is through an acquisition. Even then, a change in ownership is more likely to weaken them (difficulties with postmerger integration are well documented and, more often than not, end up destroying value).

Strategic assets are a product of a company's history. They include a wide range of intangibles such as research and development (R&D), brand and logo, know-how, collective capabilities, management and business processes, culture, employee commitment, talent management, technology beyond what may be patented, and customer loyalty and experience. As complex ecosystems have become more important, so have relational and network-embedded strategic assets. Indeed, a company may be more valuable through who its management knows and the reputation it enjoys in a network or value constellation than from what it produces!

Sometimes, strategic assets have been deliberately assembled or built in the context of a preexisting strategic vision. The famous synergy map that Walt Disney drew in 1957, sketching how the various businesses of the company would interact, support, and leverage each other in the future is a good example.[2] (Interestingly, although Disney's strategic assets have evolved since 1957, the essence of their relationships remains the same today as it did over half a century ago.)

In other cases, strategic assets have been purposefully developed as a strategic lever or wedge, providing a cornerstone to strategic advantage. Southwest Airlines, which is well known for reducing the ground servicing turnaround time of its planes in order to maximize the number of hours they fly and earn revenue every day, is a case in point. Reportedly, Southwest's cofounder Herb Kelleher even took his executives to observe and study Ferrari's Formula One team to learn how they minimized the time cars spent in pit stops during Grand Prix races. The know-how Southwest has developed over the years allows it to keep its planes in the air about 14 hours a day, which is considerably more than the average of 10 hours of revenue-generating flying that most of its competitors achieve.

But not all strategic assets are developed with a clear strategic plan in mind. Sometimes they just result from thoughtful but improvisational reactions to competition over time. Surprising as it may be, IKEA's success was not born of a master plan but stems largely from imaginative responses to a series of very practical challenges. IKEA founder Ingvar Kamprad started out as a traveling salesman, and in the late 1960s, he recognized an unserved market for simple and affordable furniture primarily among Sweden's young adults who were setting up their first homes. Kamprad designed and built some furniture aimed at this market, but the city center furniture shops that focused on up-market chic Scandinavian design had no interest in his pieces. After numerous rejections, he hit on the idea of a mail-order catalog to reach his target consumers—and so the ubiquitous IKEA catalog was born.

By the 1970s, with the suburbs around Swedish cities growing and car ownership on the rise, Kamprad saw the opportunity to add to his catalog business and establish his first store in Stockholm's outskirts. On opening, the store attracted so many customers that the checkout and warehouse staff were overwhelmed. To avoid a bottleneck creating chaos, the store manager opened the warehouse to shoppers so that they could collect their own furniture. This worked well, and IKEA's self-service concept was born from serendipitous improvisation.

The Dynamics of Strategic Assets

Regardless of how they originally came about, strategic assets are dynamic—they change over time. In companies that genuinely focus on growth and renewal, investment in scaling up existing strategic assets or developing new ones is recognized as essential to meeting strategic needs in response to changing contexts. And these companies know that strong dynamic strategic assets are a source of competitive advantage not only today but in the future. To make our discussion of the dynamic aspects of strategic assets more tangible, let's look at a simple but visible example that we recently researched: LEGO.

The name "LEGO" is an abbreviation of two Danish words: *leg godt*, meaning "play well." The company was started in 1932 in Billund, in northern Denmark, by Ole Kirk Kristiansen, a penniless carpenter who couldn't afford to buy Christmas presents for his children, so he gave them wood blocks that he designed and made himself. The blocks could be piled up to build various structures. A hit with his own children, soon after he also started selling them, and a small business took off.

After World War II, with the availability of plastics and precision molding, Kristiansen was able to create blocks that would stick together. And it was found that not only were they fun to build with, but they had all kinds of cognitive and motor development benefits for young children. As LEGO's brightly colored plastic blocks spread around the world, the LEGO brand—one of the strongest global toy brands—became a strategic asset.

LEGO blocks were manufactured using machines of the company's own design to achieve an extremely precise fit—so they could be assembled and disassembled easily by small children yet hold together well. The keys to this technical balancing act—the specifications of the plastic raw material that is hard enough for extreme precision in manufacturing but not too hard or breakable—are LEGO-specific and kept secret. This know-how is another strategic asset and a source of competitive advantage essential to the sustained attractiveness of LEGO's core product.

As LEGO designed and introduced more and more kits, it encountered a few bumps and had to develop a sophisticated logistics and supply chain process, which became a third major strategic asset, beyond the brand and manufacturing. The creativity and innovation that became a hallmark of LEGO's secretive R&D lab on its Billund campus further added to the firm's cache of strategic assets.

Looking to adjacent areas for growth, LEGO's management saw the importance of capitalizing on the emergence of media and digital entertainment. It developed alliances around movie themes and characters, first with Time Warner on Star Wars, then with Disney, among others. With the advent of gaming as a growing sector, LEGO extended its alliances into this space and, most recently, into "fluid play"—combining physical LEGO sets (say, a medieval castle kit) with virtual reality moving characters (for example, knights in a tournament or princesses going to a ball). This rich and evolving portfolio of alliances added yet another strategic asset.

Naturally, dynamism works both ways. Not only can a company's stock of strategic assets be strengthened, built on, and adapted over time in line with a changing business model, but valuable strategic assets can inadvertently be squandered and destroyed through a fatal combination of ignorance and underinvestment. When a company is in the midst of the growth curse and the CEO is focused on delivering short-term quarterly earnings, strategic assets become very vulnerable to the type of rapid decay from which it is difficult to recover.

To safeguard the future of the firm, boards and executives need to ask the following questions: Do the company's strategic assets fit with the current strategy? How might they keep, increase, or lose their value in the face of external disruption and change? Which assets have the possibility to be leveraged and repositioned for new customers, partners, or emerging business models? And how do they need to be managed so that they align with the strategic direction set by the board?

Challenges in Assessing Strategic Assets

The importance of the board being able to assess a company's strategic assets can't be overstated. According to most estimates, intangible assets (many of which will be strategic assets) now account for around two-thirds of the stock market valuation of S&P 500 firms. And service businesses, which rely heavily on strategic assets, account for 70 percent of the gross domestic product of developed countries' economies. So the move to a knowledge-based and data-driven economy means that strategic assets are likely to play an even more critical role in the future. Yet assessing strategic assets in light of a firm's strategy and strategic direction is not as straightforward as it might at first seem.

Thanks to US accounting standards inherited from a bygone age, internally generated value-creating strategic assets are treated as expenses and not recognized as assets in the same way that fixed or tangible assets are.[3] Not only does this discourage management from investing in strategic assets—as this would impact the bottom line in the short term—but it also makes valuing the investments made over time in building intangible strategic assets harder to trace and assess accurately.

The usual methods for assessing assets fall short in the case of strategic assets. Consider the most basic one: replacement value. This may work for valuing a chemical plant or a fleet of trucks, but even then, it gives rise to issues of depreciation, modernization, and the like—most of us have experienced this difficulty firsthand when dealing with insurance companies over claims for personal goods. So replacement value does not work for unique intangible assets any more than it does for a museum collection. The Tobin's Q ratio, which measures the differences between the replacement value of physical assets and the stock market valuation of a company, is a crude instrument that can tell us little about intangible strategic assets. Another method, market value, based on how much the asset could be sold for, cannot easily be applied to strategic assets, either—recall that one of their four defining characteristics is that they are not tradable!

A paradox arises in that the more an intangible asset has strategic value, the less easily its value can be assessed. In researching strategic alliances, and considering what partners brought to and would expect to gain from specific alliances, we developed

Figure 9.1: The Paradox of Valuing Strategic Assets

a simple list of asset types (see figure 9.1) that reflects this and may provide a starting point.

The list is constructed so that the least tangible but perhaps most critical strategic assets appear at the bottom. Some are extremely hard to assess but may well be the most vital. In a discussion with Paolo Fresco, a former head of GE Europe, we were reminiscing about the origins of the company's extremely successful jet engine alliance with SNECMA (now part of Safran Group, the French engine and aircraft equipment manufacturer) and the fact that, in Fresco's view, the most uniquely valuable strategic assets brought to the alliance by SNECMA were the close relationships the company's leadership enjoyed with key decision makers and stakeholders in governments, the military, and the aviation industry in Europe at a critical time when Airbus was being launched.

Beyond an enticing label that denotes their importance, strategic assets remain hard to assess because they are often only revealed in action. So, for instance, ahead of collaborating with SNECMA, GE had no way of verifying how important the French group's relational strategic assets really were. It had to enter the alliance based on trust, and only through the process of collaboration was the value of SNECMA's relationships with stakeholders and customers in Europe revealed.

Assessing Strategic Assets

If standard valuation methods are not sufficient for assessing the strength of strategic assets, we need to look to other approaches that can provide insight into different types of strategic assets.

Partners—The Looking Glass

Industry convergence and platform approaches highlight the increasing importance of strategic alliances and ecosystems. Close alliance partners should be well positioned to offer an accurate and honest assessment of your partnering strategic assets. Occasionally, the value of specific strategic assets lies in the eye of the beholder, meaning partners will more likely recognize the true importance and worth of these assets.

A few years ago, we were asked to do a quick assessment of a company's strengths in relation to partnering. We interviewed executives at the company and were given access to a wide range of internal documents—all of which collectively provided a consistent and positive picture. It was clear that executives regarded the firm's partnering skills as a strong strategic asset. But we also surveyed the company's partners, and this process unearthed a strikingly different and disturbing view. As outlined in figure 9.2, every strength the company's leadership had identified as

How We See Ourselves	*How Our Partners See Us*
High quality	Rely on brand/image
Reliable	Rigid
Predictable	Stubborn
Decisive	Autocratic
Share our good work	Impose solutions
Analytical	Insensitive
Experts	Overly specialized
Technically the best	Too expensive
Systematic	Slow & inefficient

Figure 9.2: The Other Side of the Looking Glass

a strategic asset in its alliances, its strategic partners viewed, with skepticism, as a weakness.

Wildly differing views on the strength and effectiveness of strategic assets are more likely to emerge when the company being assessed is large and dominant, and when its size, strength, and a good helping of hubris tend to reinforce a positive, top-of-the-food-chain perspective. Seeking out the input of alliance or ecosystem partners who will give a candid and critical assessment of how they see you as a partner may well be an eye-opening and useful exercise.

Customers and Complementors

The quality and sustainability of relationships with customers needs to be considered as a source of future advantage (or not). Quality may matter more for the future than quantity today, as a large installed base with poor customer appreciation makes a company deeply vulnerable. Tools such as customer-based corporate valuation (CBCV) focus on the loyalty of customers as a source of sustainable advantage—by tracking customer acquisition rates, customer retention, the frequency of transactions per customer, and the expenditure per purchase—and arguably provide a relatively clear assessment of customers as a strategic asset.[4]

With the growth of ecosystem-based business models, complementors also play an increasingly important role in a company's portfolio of strategic assets. Keeping complementors aligned, committed, and loyal is vital, so seeking their views on your company's products, services, and processes can flag early-warning signs of trouble to come. In 2010, for instance, Nokia's Symbian mobile operating system still enjoyed the largest installed base in the world by a wide margin. As far as Nokia's leaders were concerned, customers were happy and all was well. But the company's Achilles' heel lay elsewhere—with the increasingly important community of application developers. It took much longer for developers to master Symbian's intricacies than it did for them to learn how to develop applications on the new emerging operating systems of Apple and Google. Someone considering this carefully would have seen the writing on the wall, but Nokians were not used to looking at complementors' pain points, and they had not yet fully grasped the difficult nature of multisided markets.[5] When developers began abandoning Nokia, this had a knock-on effect on the company's once-loyal customer base, as its new rivals offered customers many more apps than Nokia could.

Supply Chain

The world isn't short of supply chain consultants armed with various metrics against which the optimization, stability, and resilience of a supply chain can be judged. But to be considered a valuable strategic asset, a supply chain has to offer something more. It has to be a genuine source of competitive advantage that allows a company to continually adapt, particularly to unforeseen risks and "black swan" events, such as the COVID pandemic or war in Ukraine.[6] According to a McKinsey study, since 2020, the risk of supply chain disruption due to a range of risks, from climate change and cyberattacks to trade disputes and pandemics, has grown steadily, with costly supply chain disruptions of more than two months occurring, on average, just short of every five years.[7]

So what might constitute a supply chain that is a strong strategic asset? Again, the IKEA example is instructive. IKEA has built a highly unusual supplier network. Instead of turning to furniture manufacturers as suppliers, IKEA sought out a variety of specialist companies to supply high-volume, standardized individual elements for its modular-designed pieces—nuts and bolts, engineered wood, textiles, and so on. Initially, this approach was to keep costs down, but over time, it became critical to protecting IKEA designs and know-how from competitors. Where it could, IKEA tried to select producers in seasonal markets, such as ski and toy manufacturers, allowing it to use their off-season idle capacity at a discount, thereby reducing the cost of its own products. One of the reasons IKEA has been so dominant for so long in the segment it created is because its strong, efficient, globally sourced supply chain makes it impossible for competitors to copy.

To understand the value of a supply chain as a strategic asset, it should be looked at with fresh eyes while asking the following questions: Does our supply chain have the resilience to adapt to mitigate external disruptions? Does our supply chain continually evolve to exploit new opportunities? And is our supply chain unique enough to be a source of competitive advantage?

Dynamic Capabilities

An assessment of strategic assets should also consider higher-order dynamic capabilities.[8] These can be a hodgepodge of managerial skills and capabilities that make a difference and ultimately contribute to the strategic agility of a firm through the ability of managers to anticipate, interpret, and respond to evolving demands effectively.

To make this more tangible, let's consider Cisco. For decades now, Cisco has been the leading maker of internet routers and other related internet connectivity hardware. Cisco has maintained its leadership largely through a dynamic capability to identify, approach, acquire, and integrate promising innovative technology start-ups and retain their technical and managerial talent. In short, it has developed the skills to essentially outsource R&D and innovation and integrate the outcomes. But this type of dynamic capability can only flourish with a well-functioning talent management system in place to ensure the flow of competent and motivated managers.

Too Broad or Too Narrow

Moving on from assessing specific types of strategic assets to taking a wider view, it is useful to consider the breadth and applicability of a firm's strategic assets. The easiest way to think about this is by looking at two companies with strategic assets at the extremes of this spectrum. At one extreme, HP developed a set of very broad strategic assets that could be distributed across many individual businesses with different customer bases and channels. But these were not strong or unique enough to provide a source of differentiation for HP. And so the company found itself competing across a range of different segments without being able to build or leverage its strategic assets to gain significant competitive advantage in any; consequently, HP left itself vulnerable to disruptions in all of those segments.

At the other extreme, the Timken Company built highly focused and specialized strategic assets that gave it global leadership in the subcategory of tapered roller bearings. Although Timken was unmatched in product quality, innovation, and durability and its strategic assets were extremely strong, they were so specific to one narrow field that redeploying or redirecting the assets toward strategic change would be extremely challenging.

Even though HP and Timken represent the opposite ends of the spectrum—one with broad, weak strategic assets and the other with strong, specialized ones—ultimately the nature of their strategic assets could lead to the same position: neither being able to respond quickly enough to disruption or major change in their industry or having enough flexibility for long-term renewal.

An important element in the assessment of strategic assets is looking at how focused, applicable, and potentially flexible they are. Are they so broad and general that they provide no real competitive advantage? Are they so specific to the requirements of our current business that redirecting them would be difficult? Or are they strong and unique enough for today while also having the flexibility to be developed to support the strategic direction of the company?

Do We Invest Adequately in Strategic Assets?

As we saw in chapter 7, a breakdown in the strategy process doesn't manifest itself in strategy failure and financial crisis for many years. And boards need to be aware of a similar lag in relation to strategic assets. Underinvestment in R&D and innovation, brand and marketing, staff and management training, partners and relationships will weaken strategic assets but will not immediately lead to a decline in company performance.

As we also saw in chapter 3, under shareholder pressure to increase returns, the quickest and easiest route for the executive is to cut expenses—even though these expense items are often the very same strategic assets that are critical to a company's renewal, long-term survival, and prosperity. This speaks directly to the board's mandate to safeguard the future of the company for all stakeholders and as part of meeting that mandate, the board should monitor investment in a company's key strategic assets to get a sense of whether they are strengthening or eroding. When the board puts investment in strategic assets in the spotlight, this will hopefully have the added benefit of sparing strategic assets from coming under the axe as a quick fix to restore the balance sheet the next time the CEO feels under pressure from investors.

Strategic Liabilities

An assessment of strategic assets isn't complete without addressing their more problematic siblings: strategic liabilities. These are costly, hard to compensate for or offset, and can result in irremediable competitive weaknesses. This can be seen vividly in the case of SNCF, the French railroad provider. With the

European Union encouraging competition to challenge old monopolies, SNCF has found itself on the backfoot, scrambling to overhaul its people management processes—a strategic liability relic dating from post-WWII nationalization that has been hijacked by militant unions (which have brought their workers out on strike every year since 1947).

Not all strategic liabilities result from the past choices, decisions, or histories of a firm, though. Some may be external and outside the company's control, which makes them particularly dangerous, especially when strategic choices are made with them in mind. Take, for instance, Swissair. The company was long a model of quality and reliability that other airlines sought to emulate. Yet, in 2002, Swissair became the victim of a combination of strategic liabilities outside its control and the decisions it had made to overcome them. It abruptly ceased operations and went into bankruptcy.

The first external strategic liability facing Swissair was the fact it was the flag carrier of a small country surrounded by many large neighbors. The second was that it was not part of the European Union (EU). Consequently, Swissair faced restricted access to European skies, made worse when a dispute between the European Union and Switzerland over air pollution (caused by European trucks passing through Switzerland) resulted in additional air traffic restrictions being imposed on Switzerland.

To overcome these external strategic liabilities, Swissair sought to expand its scope through long-haul global alliances with Delta and Singapore Airlines. But neither partner was satisfied with the European traffic volume Swissair brought them. And in an effort to generate more traffic and surmount its non-EU, single-hub disadvantage, Swissair entered into a series of alliances with smaller European airlines (some were flag carriers in other small countries, others secondary airlines in bigger countries). Swissair also purchased large numbers of planes and leased them to its European partners with an agreement that Swissair would provide the technical maintenance and other support services for the leased fleets from its Swiss base.

Unfortunately for Swissair, a third external strategic liability made its situation even worse: The rising value of the Swiss franc made the labor costs of the maintenance and support contracts prohibitive, and many of its partners reneged on their agreements. But even before this, Swissair found that instead of its partners collaborating, many of them were working in direct competition with the company over lucrative long-haul networks.

Not only was Swissair disadvantaged by Switzerland's small size, being outside the European Union, and having a strong currency, but it faced a fourth external strategic liability in the country's topography. Having a very mountainous terrain made it impossible to expand its hub airport in Zurich. When the French government announced it would enlarge Charles de Gaulle Airport giving Air France a strategic asset to build a hub operation, both of Swissair's long-haul partners deserted it, and Delta joined Air France in the SkyTeam alliance.

As the example of Swissair clearly shows, external strategic liabilities expose firms to more competitive attacks. They can foreclose some strategic growth options such as acquisitions or ambitious international development. And they can result in firms making poor strategic choices in a bid to overcome the external strategic liabilities that are beyond their control.

With regard to strategic liabilities, there are two important lessons for the board:

First, be aware of a company's legacy strategic liabilities because they could seriously impede both the strategic direction set by the board and the successful implementation of the CEO's near-term strategy.

Second, sketch out a map of external strategic liabilities (here, experts from a range a backgrounds with a systems thinking approach could help). Understanding what these external strategic liabilities are and the limitations they may impose on strategic options today and in the future is critical to a firm's long-term viability and success.

Strategic Assets in a Multibusiness Firm

For the sake of (relative) simplicity, so far we have focused on strategic assets in single-product or single-business firms. Diversified companies add further challenges. First, it is even harder for directors and corporate executives to assess the health and value-adding contribution of strategic assets of several different businesses rather than just one—particularly as some may be shared and some may be specific to an individual business. Second, mapping which strategic assets can be leveraged across different businesses as a basis for growth is a difficult task that requires time, collaboration, diplomacy, and trust (as the results can easily be interpreted as revealing business unit winners and losers). And finally, in a healthy multibusiness firm, corporate ought to provide a number of group-wide strategic assets that should not be duplicated by individual businesses.

One of the strategic advantages of a diversified company should be the provision of corporate-level strategic assets of a quality and cost that might not be available to the individual businesses if they were on their own. These range from better financing (higher credit ratings, lower interest rates on debt, more leverage with the parent's guarantee) to better human resources (the ability to attract better trained and more experienced managers and offer them further career development prospects) and tighter management processes and disciplines. This was the formula of old-style conglomerates, such as Hanson Trust in the United Kingdom or ITT in the United States. It remains a key part of how private equity investment groups create value. And in its heyday, GE too was renowned for providing this type of value to its various businesses in the form of strategic planning tools, quality management, and financial engineering.

How each business within a portfolio is able to access strategic assets matters. Which strategic assets are public—available to all businesses within the group—and which are treated as private assets by individual businesses? At 3M, for instance, the 35 technology platforms that make up the core of 3M's technical leadership are clearly corporate property and treated as public assets accessible to all product divisions, whereas customer relationships and partners are treated as private assets belonging to each business group. Divisions may collaborate to serve common customers, but that decision is up to them.

How brands and logos are shared can bring both advantages and disadvantages. When strong and consistent brands are used across a portfolio of companies, such as in Richard Branson's Virgin Group, brand value and reputation become very valuable strategic assets. But this is only as long as all companies using the brand perform well and stay free from scandal or trouble. It takes just one business group using the brand to encounter problems for the entire brand to be tarnished and become a strategic liability.

But strategic assets in diversified companies extend beyond what is provided by corporate. Learning, capabilities, know-how, and data created within individual businesses all become much more valuable assets when leveraged across the group. Chinese company Ping An, for instance, has mastered the art of algorithms and knowledge graphs that allow the integrated analysis of hitherto separate "data lakes" from its five key business areas: finance, healthcare, smart cities, real estate, and autos. This gives Ping An's businesses a fuller and more holistic picture of individual customers and allows different businesses to provide targeted offerings. So, for example, its Autohome online vehicle sales platform leverages years of data from the financing and insurance groups to offer tailored loans and insurance to each customer, something none of its competitors are able to do.[9]

A basic way to begin to think about strategic assets in diversified firms is sketched out in figure 9.3. Clearly, what's

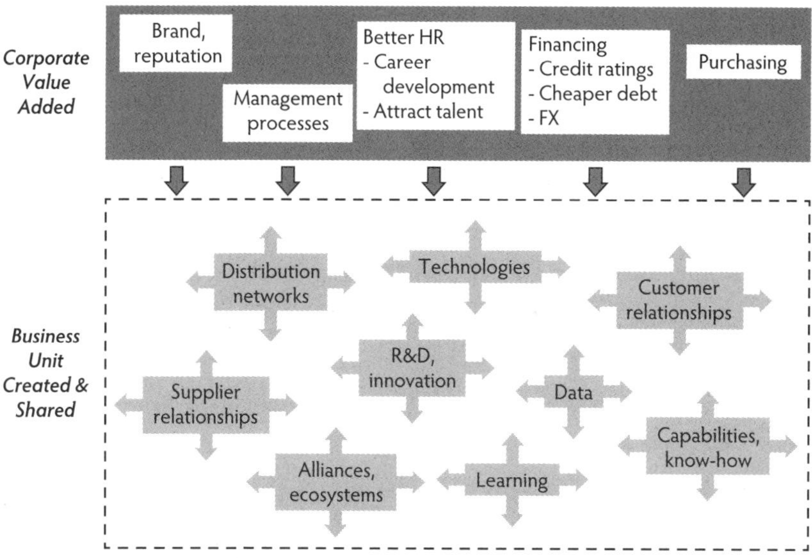

Figure 9.3: Are Strategic Assets Common across the Group?

important here is not only the extent to which corporate strategic assets are leveraged across different businesses but whether strategic assets created within individual businesses are leveraged across the group. Identifying and mapping strategic assets at the corporate and individual business levels will also highlight gaps and opportunities of where assets could be shared between specific businesses to strengthen and develop the capabilities and flexibility needed to help the company toward its strategic direction.

Assessing Corporate Coherence

In multibusiness companies, corporate coherence is a higher-level strategic asset. It is the logic and advantage of each individual business being part of the group. And a lack of corporate coherence is the thing that keeps directors and CEOs awake at night, watching for the wolves at the door as ever more vocal activist shareholders call for the breakup of companies that they argue would have more value as standalone businesses or as part of another diversified group.

When thinking about the degree to which corporate coherence provides a strategic asset across a multibusiness group, there are three fundamental questions to bear in mind:

- Are key activities similar, whether internally (such as key business processes) or externally oriented (brand and quality reputation)?
- Are customer, supplier, and partner relationships across businesses of a similar nature?
- Are the underlying business logics similar across businesses, and are key variables and success factors affecting performance of a similar nature?

If the answer to these questions is yes, this allows corporate management and directors to develop comparable cognitive maps and common attention rules to the most important variables one needs to pay attention to. In other words, it allows them to shift from considering one business to considering another, relatively easily. If the answer is no, coherence will be lower, making corporate management's task of adding value much more difficult. The risk of a "dominant logic" from one business being applied across the entire portfolio will likely increase—and this is a perilous situation that reduces flexibility, agility, and the strategic options of each of the businesses in the firm.

If corporate coherence is weak, the board and executive are confronted with difficult choices: either keep the more diverse portfolio, with corporate making a lower contribution to the value creation of the group (and risk the activists forcing your hand), or streamline the portfolio to focus on fewer businesses that have the potential for stronger corporate value creation (and risk shareholder wrath in the short term).

Strategic Assets and Available Choices

We have seen in this chapter the importance of being able to assess the state of a company's strategic assets, and if we use the analogy of a card game, they are part of the hand you have been dealt. Every aspect of strategy the board deals with, from the strategic dialogue it has with the executive team to the strategic direction it sets, will be affected by the firm's strategic assets. Are they overextended or underleveraged? Is the company too thinly spread and its strategy excessively ambitious, given its strategic assets? Or is it underexploiting its assets, too conservative, overly risk averse, and probably missing opportunities?

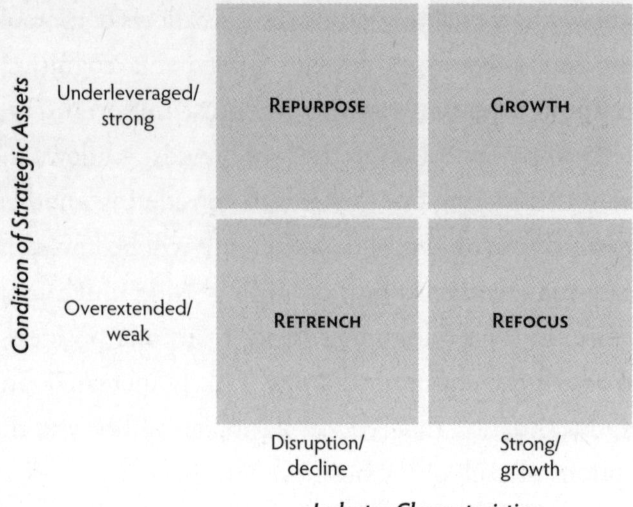

Figure 9.4: Impact of Strategic Assets and Industry Positions on Strategic Options

As illustrated in figure 9.4, the answers to these questions and the resulting strategic choices available to a company depend to a large extent on the condition of the industry in which it operates—whether the industry is facing disruption and decline or is strong and growing.

Disrupted industry and overextended strategic assets—The predicament for a company with weak or overextended strategic assets in an industry that is facing disruption or decline is more than likely untenable. Retrenchment is inevitable, and with very limited strategic options available, the company may stumble into bankruptcy before a managed contraction is underway.

Strong industry and overextended strategic assets—A company trying to compete with weak or overextended strategic assets in a strong industry more than likely finds itself in this position because its strategy process has broken down, it is heading toward a crisis, and its leadership has been overly focused on managing the bottom line instead of managing the firm's health—in other words, the company has fallen victim to the growth curse. This doesn't have to be a terminal position, though, as opportunities clearly exist in the industry.

For a company in this position, the board's role is two-fold. First, it can help the executive identify where to re-focus the firm (as a smaller, more agile player), using the strategic direction as a guide to renewal opportunities. Second, the board should very publicly support the CEO (as IBM's board did when Ginni Rometty embarked on re-building the company's strategic assets to refocus on new growth opportunities—which we discuss in more detail in chapter 10). Refocusing a company and strengthening the relevant strategic assets takes time, guts, and usually a few years of poor financial results—a process that needs to be clearly communicated to shareholders so that the CEO isn't distracted by unhelpful noise about the firm's financial performance vis-à-vis its stronger peers.

Disrupted industry and underleveraged strategic assets—From this position, it is possible to repurpose underleveraged strategic assets, exit existing core businesses, and put a company on the path of renewal. This is exactly what happened to Fujifilm. With the analog film industry in decline, new CEO Shigetaka Komori undertook an inventory of the firm's strategic assets from which he and his team identified six potential new growth areas, including medical systems, life sciences, and optical devices. Over the next decade,

Fujifilm went through the painful process of exiting its core business, restructuring to reflect the new business domains, and investing significantly in strengthening and repositioning its strategic assets. This type of repurposing calls for bold leadership and a board of directors strong and patient enough to step in and shield the CEO from shareholder pressure while the transformation is underway.

Strong industry and underleveraged strategic assets— Certainly the strongest position to be in, prudently underleveraged strategic assets in a strong industry will support continual renewal, allowing a company to extend into new market positions and potentially shape new segments. But because no industry is stable forever, the board needs to keep an eye out for potential disruptions on the horizon and maintain a dialogue with the executive about how the firm's strategic assets might fare in light of upcoming changes and inflection points.

■

To recap, strategic assets are one of the core building blocks of the strategic options open to a company both in the long and short term. The board's strategic direction has to be rooted in the strategic assets the company possesses—if these assets are weak or missing, there is little chance of realizing that ambition. And as far as the near-term strategy is concerned, the state of strategic assets and how they are leveraged dictates not only the options available but the robustness and flexibility of the strategy in the face of disruptions and change. But when strategic assets, which have taken years to develop, are sacrificed on the altar of excessive operational efficiency for short-term results, this creates damaging vulnerabilities, from which it can be difficult to recover.

10 ∎ Strategic Agility and Strategic Options

The strategic options open to a company today are probably narrower than they once were simply because increased speed and cycle times give firms less time to build the new capabilities and accumulate the strategic assets they might need to pursue certain strategies. Thinking back to the analogy of a card game, companies have to play the hand they have been dealt—and chapter 9 explained how strategic assets make up an important part of that hand. But the three vectors of strategic agility also play a critical role in determining the strength or

This chapter is derived from ideas developed by Andrea Cuomo, who in turn was inspired by the earlier work of Yves Doz and Mikko Kosonen as summarized in their book *Fast Strategy: How Strategic Agility Will Help You Stay Ahead of the Game* (Philadelphia: Wharton School Publishing, 2008).

weakness of the company's hand. And it is vital that the board understand the relative health of these vectors and how they interact because they impact a company's ambition for growth in the short and long term.

We have already introduced leadership unity and strategic sensitivity—two of the vectors of strategic agility—in relation to board directors functioning as a team and the skills and tools they require for working on the strategic direction. Now, we are going to look at the three vectors in the original context they were developed in the book *Fast Strategy*—to provide insight into whether the CEO and executive team have the capabilities to realize strategic transformation of the firm's business model.

What Is Strategic Agility?

Strategic agility is the ability to continually seek out and rapidly react to new strategic opportunities while withdrawing from mature or slowing businesses and, in so doing, avoiding falling victim to the growth curse. It is achieved from executive management's thoughtful and purposive interplay between three vectors: strategic sensitivity, leadership unity, and resource fluidity, as outlined in figure 10.1.

> *Strategic sensitivity*—This is the sharpness of perception and the intensity of awareness and attention. Heightened strategic sensitivity allows companies to anticipate disruption, be aware of the need for renewal and transformation, identify new opportunities, and make the adjustments needed to business models in order to maintain strategic advantage.

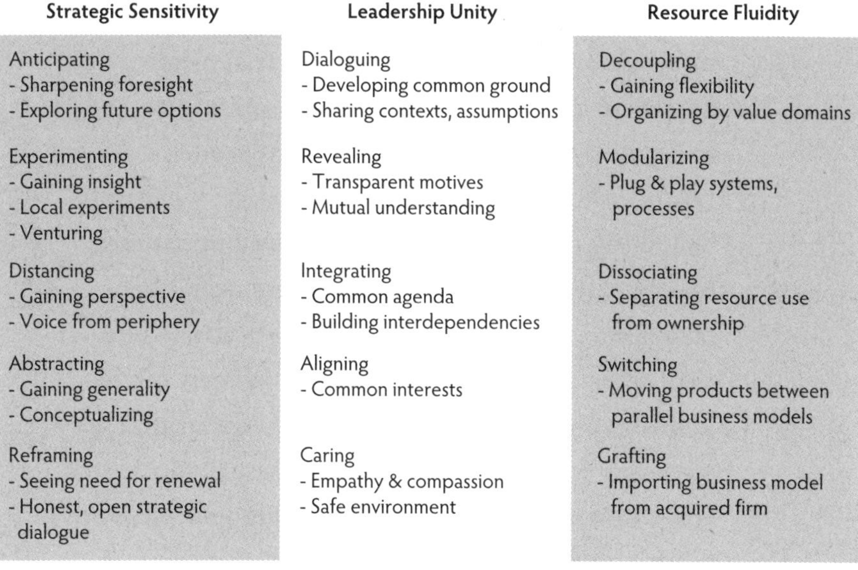

Figure 10.1: Strategic Agility—Leadership Actions

Leadership unity—This is the ability of the executive team to make bold, fast decisions. Strong leadership unity involves collective commitment, shared goals, and a powerful sense of purpose that allows for difficult and risky decisions to be made without win-lose politics coming into play. For true unity in the executive team, a degree of integration across businesses is essential, with some incentives being based on corporate rather than subunit performance.

Resource fluidity—This refers to the structural agility and processes needed to translate ideas into actions through the rapid redeployment of resources and reconfiguration of capabilities. It can be achieved by:

- Decoupling a very integrated, focused, and centralized business model into distinct and autonomous but well-coordinated entities.

- Modularizing the underlying business process and information technology systems so that elements of a business system can be quickly disassembled and reassembled to support new business models.
- Dissociating resource use from resource ownership.
- Switching products between multiple but parallel business models as businesses mature or markets change to increase flexibility and radically reduce the time it takes to migrate to new business models.
- Grafting business models, which involves acquiring a company with a very different business model that acts as a stimulus to change for existing operations. Grafting usually works best when the transition is tapered—so the new business model initially complements the old and gradually gains influence over time until it has substituted the original business model.

Assessing Strategic Agility

It is incumbent on the board to be able to gauge the strategic agility of the company. A good starting point before launching into an assessment of the levels of strategic sensitivity, leadership unity, and resource fluidity is to look for symptoms of a lack of strategic agility—or to put it another way, to think about occurrences of strategic rigidity in the company. Figure 10.2 lists the issues to look out for; they are often much easier to recognize than the dimensions outlined in figure 10.1.

Gauging the Level of Strategic Sensitivity
The degree of strategic sensitivity in a firm can be assessed indirectly through the extent to which the methods and tools we

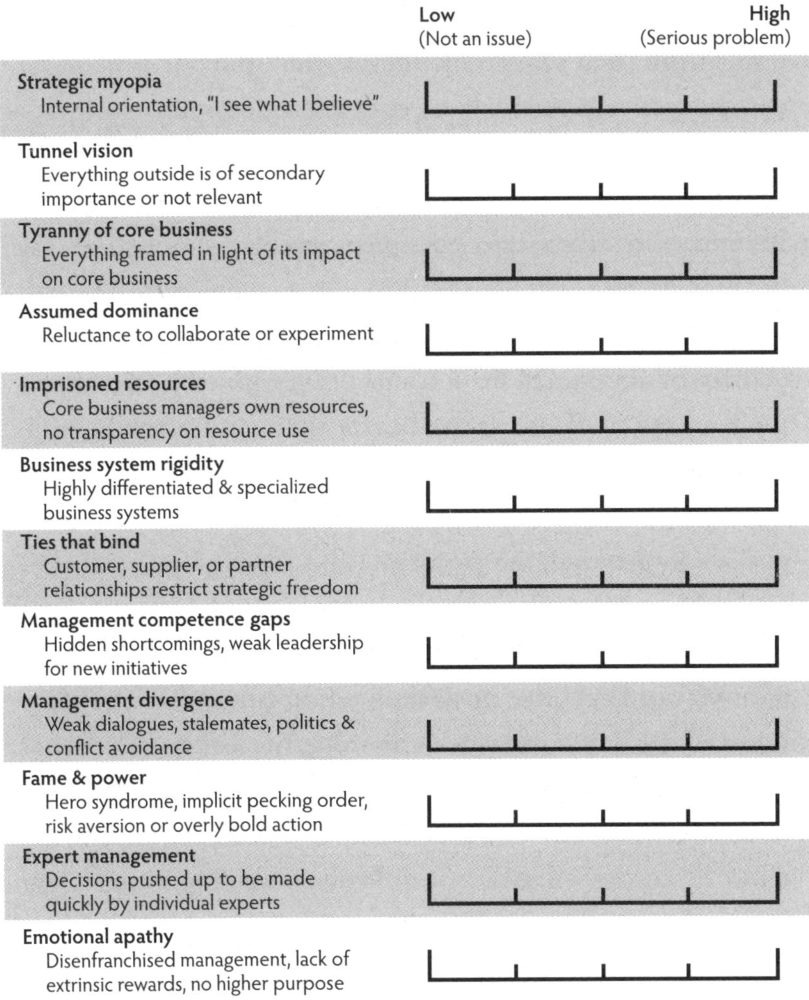

Figure 10.2: How Strategically Rigid Is Your Company?

discussed in chapter 6 are applied (foresight, anticipating in-flection points, technology scanning, forward-looking indica-tors, listening to customers, learning experiments, distancing, challenging, and reframing). While the use of these tools to in-form the strategy process does not fully guarantee the CEO and senior executive team have developed genuine strategic sensitivity, or the strategizing capabilities we would expect to result from such sensitivity, they at least provide proxies for executive management's interest in strategic issues.

Assessing Leadership Unity

In some cases, the board's assessment on this vector will be easy because the lack of leadership unity in a company will be palpable. For instance, the CEO is controlling and narcissistic; perhaps business units are in competition with each other, fighting for scarce resources; maybe the signs of a breakdown in the strategy process are apparent (think back to the indicators discussed in chapter 7); or growth has stalled, and without any options for renewal, the executive team are either panicking or in denial and shoring up the illusion of growth.

But be warned. Even when things look rosy, the appearance of unity can sometimes be misleading. In cultures of specialization and avoidance, in which criticizing the actions of others is not part of the cultural DNA of the firm, what might look like leadership unity can in fact be far from it in reality. In this scenario, executives will avoid the difficult conversations that might lead to them having to challenge each other, and so, for all intents and purposes, everyone will appear to be singing from the same hymn sheet. But under stress, this facade will break.

Even the best cultures of generalized reciprocity (give before you take, and trust that someone in the organization will help you when you are in need) will likely fray under pressure. Highly interdependent business models and organizational processes that make individual success dependent on everyone else's are more structurally resilient, but they can also be more vulnerable to individual or subunit weaknesses.

Understanding the Conditions for Resource Fluidity

Most actions of strategic significance are likely to require resources and call for difficult resource allocation choices. But there is an inherent challenge to resource fluidity, due to the nature of what economists call "private" or sticky resources. That is, once resources are allocated to implementing a particular set of priorities, they are no longer available for use elsewhere. These resources are most often capital, investment, and management attention. So the scarcity of private resources leads to tensions and results in their allocation, more often than not, becoming a political process in which there are distinct winners and losers.

As companies mature and growth stalls, it's common for internal competition to become even more intense, with subunit managers competing for scarce resources. In some contexts, large and successful businesses can dominate resource allocation decisions and starve new initiatives that would build the future. At Microsoft, for instance, the dominance of the Windows operating system stifled and delayed renewal initiatives and fostered a harsh culture of conflict for many years. Indian academics and executives liken this approach to a banyan tree: It brings the advantage that its size offers protection from the sun, but there is a downside in that it lets nothing grow around it. And this is exactly the type of resource allocation process that traps large, mature companies in the growth curse.

Even organizational structures that were designed to foster resource fluidity often deliver the opposite—stalemates and inaction. The ominous but well-known and often painfully felt phrase "matrix paralysis" reminds us of this pitfall. Unless resource allocation processes in the matrix are well honed and seen as legitimate by all, the resource allocation flexibility offered by a matrix organization may turn into a nightmare.

A conflictual and political resource allocation process corrupts culture throughout an organization (not just in corporate entities, but we see this in public administrations too, with departments fighting for a slice of ever-diminishing budgets). Pitting one group against another in a competition for resources obviously destroys the likelihood of internal collaboration, increases instances of misrepresentation, and creates a climate in which it is impossible to have leadership unity. From this type of conflictual process, there are only two possible outcomes, neither of which is good news for long-term prospects. Either the company goes into stasis, or it enters a spiral of decline in which significant damage is done before any problems become evident to the outside world (recall from chapter 7 how long the journey of decline is from a breakdown in the strategy process to a financial crisis).

The Three Vectors in Concert

There is obviously value in the board understanding the state of the individual vectors of strategic sensitivity, leadership unity, and resource fluidity in the firm, as a weakness in any of these indicates potential problems brewing that must be addressed. And having that knowledge is one of the many factors that differentiates leading from lagging boards. However, greater insight comes from analyzing the interplay between the three vectors. This will reveal the degree of readiness and flexibility in a firm—the strategic agility—and what can and cannot realistically be achieved.

Strong strategic sensitivity, for instance, results in a better cognitive understanding of what future options may or may not be available to pursue. Yet strategic sensitivity alone obviously won't suffice. It would lead to a widening gap between awareness and action—the "knowing-doing gap" that Jeff Pfeffer and Robert Sutton warned us against.[1] This would breed frustration, cynicism, and discouragement, resulting in the better talent probably exiting the company.

It is only when the vectors are well orchestrated and employed in concert that the opportunities to shape the company's future actually become feasible. To get to effective action, strong leadership unity is paramount because sharp strategic sensitivity needs to be shared and discussed by the executive team and lead to a strong commitment to action. But that commitment to action, critical to leadership unity, is meaningless without resource fluidity. If resources are trapped or owned by individual businesses and the resource allocation process is combative, then by the time the requisite resources have been mobilized to support a new initiative, it will be a case of too little too late.

The direct interdependency between strategic sensitivity and resource fluidity is less intuitively obvious, but it is equally critical. Strategic sensitivity provides a much-needed strategic context. It creates a window through which an understanding of the company's predicament can be viewed, and this extends to the challenges facing each business unit. This shared understanding underpins a fluid resource allocation process; without it, politics and self-interest would dictate where the firm's resources were deployed.

SAP's transformation from a product developer to platform-based ecosystem player provides a good illustration of how each of the vectors are needed to build a strategically agile company capable of renewal and transformation. Back in 2006, after intense strategy dialogues, SAP's leaders responded to the potential threat of the internet by refocusing the company on a new internet-based platform with three main domains: business processes open to third-party application developers; mid-market clients (that is, small and medium-sized enterprises, whereas previously its clients were mostly Fortune 1000 firms); and better customer value through what SAP called a "service-oriented architecture" that allowed customers to create new applications and seamlessly integrate them with SAP's offering.

Together, SAP's then CEO, Henning Kagermann, and co-founder and chairman, Hasso Plattner, began strengthening the company's strategic sensitivity with the hiring of a new cadre of young and bright senior executives—mostly from the United States and based in Palo Alto. These "outsiders" would bring a fresh perspective on the industry to counter the many baby boomers in the senior ranks at SAP's headquarters in Germany. In a radical move to support resource fluidity, executive team roles were reorganized to focus on contributions to the value chain rather than individual businesses. This enabled rapid resource reallocation to wherever resources were needed to support the development of the new platform and the enterprise services being hosted on it.

For the new strategy to work, stronger communication, collaboration, and employee engagement were key, and much of this would flow from leadership unity. The executive team reaffirmed SAP's foundational values of customer focus, quality, engineering excellence, integrity, commitment, and passion but added new priorities as well: agility, simplicity, high performance, global collaboration, and talent development. These were not treated as a set of slogans to be publicly announced and almost immediately overlooked but became the guiding principles to drive culture throughout the company and prepare SAP for the future.

Assessing Strategic Options

Obviously, true agility comes from being in the ideal position of having high levels of strategic sensitivity, leadership unity, and resource fluidity. This offers a vast range of strategic options, but very few companies find themselves in this advantaged place. For most companies, though, the quality of the position of a business on each of the three vectors will limit the options available. It is up to the board to assess the relative strength of each vector and then evaluate the CEO's near-term strategy proposals and, more widely, the company's readiness to successfully navigate disruptions, inflection points, and growth options based on its analysis. Figure 10.3 illustrates this in a simple form.

Let's first take the positions of strategic sensitivity and leadership unity. Strong strategic sensitivity allows you to identify future developments and anticipate them with greater confidence. Combined with strong leadership unity and genuine collective commitment, you will be able to pursue these developments with an appreciation of risks involved. Rather than singling out scapegoats for failed experiments or discouraging them altogether, the senior leadership team will assume collective responsibility for bold moves.

Conversely, limited strategic sensitivity and lack of leadership unity make proactive anticipatory moves unfeasible. The company can only be a "blind follower," copying what more strategically aware competitors do and finding reassurance in the fact that these competitors pave the way. Unless you have superior

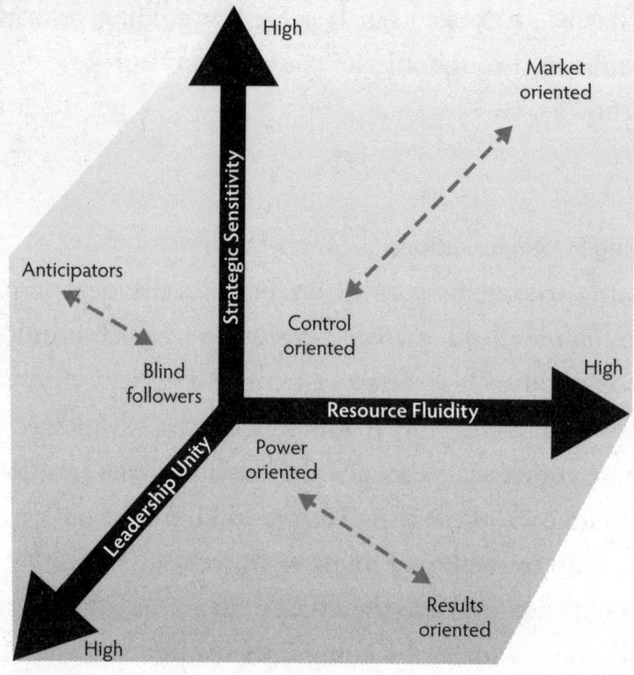

Figure 10.3: Vectors of Strategic Agility

strategic assets and fast scale-up capabilities, this is a weak position. Strategy consultants might be brought in to provide strategic sensitivity by proxy, and a new CEO and executive team may be hired to foster more collective commitment. But this will take time, cause internal disruption, and the results will only show over time.

We can similarly consider the interactions between resource fluidity and leadership unity dependent on their relative strength or weakness. A united, results-oriented executive team will achieve resource fluidity. Their collective commitment means they are unlikely to frame decisions in the sterile win-lose political perspective that plagues power-oriented organizations—where senior executives see each other as rivals in a competition, a tournament, or even a fight for scarce resources. Conversely, weak leadership unity in the power-oriented scenario sees executives who are more likely to hoard resources or spend them beyond real needs "just in case." In this type of firm, those whose power is inherited from past successes tend to have the loudest voices. In classic growth curse behavior, they continue overinvesting in what once made the core business strong to the detriment of nurturing new opportunities. In the absence of shared strategic sensitivity and a lack of convergent understanding of priorities and constraints, this leads executives—in a competitive rather than collaborative attitude—to overemphasize resource "ownership" and control over resource access, use, and leverage.

If a board finds the company is positioned closer to the origin of our three vectors, there are unfortunately limited options, and these are dependent on the state of the company's strategic assets (as discussed in chapter 9). If strategic assets are weak and overextended, a managed retrenchment is probably the best option. However, if the firm's strategic assets are strong, under-leveraged, differentiating, and also fit for the future, the board may conclude that a new CEO and executive team could be a solution to change things for the better. Nevertheless, there is a caveat—for a change in leadership to be effective, there has to be considerable pride and pent-up energy in the rank and file of the firm. If the lack of unity at the top—the infighting and lack of strategic awareness—has penetrated the rest of the company, the task of repositioning and renewal becomes extremely difficult. Then the board needs to ask whether and to what extent the culture has been damaged. (We look at this question in more detail in chapter 11.)

A change in leadership shouldn't just be reserved for stagnating companies with low positions on all vectors, though.

Even if positions on each vector are relatively good, in some circumstances, when growth begins to slow, it may make sense to bring in new blood at the top simply because one has to account for the wear and tear inherent in running a company. In chapter 2, we stressed how difficult the role of the CEO has become, and once growth stalls, how demanding and conflicting the pressures are. To put it bluntly, no matter how successful an incumbent CEO is, it may not be ideal to have that individual take the company into the next stage of the journey.

Assessing strategic options based on the relative strengths and weaknesses of a company's strategic sensitivity, leadership unity, and resource fluidity is a complex and nuanced undertaking. And in thinking about this, we owe a debt of gratitude to our long-time collaborator and friend Andrea Cuomo of STMicro-electronics, who was the first to begin thinking about the strategic options available to mature companies based on how they fared on the three vectors of strategic agility. To get the process rolling, figure 10.4 provides a simplified representation of the possible configurations. It's worth stressing that the cube in figure 10.4 focuses on extreme "all or nothing" positions, whereas most companies will find themselves somewhere between the extremes on each of the vectors. And so the usefulness of the cube is not in being a tool to accurately plot a position and options but in providing a frame within which the board of directors can begin a dialogue with the CEO and executive team around the strategic options and the development of an action agenda.

To avoid the very pedestrian approach of walking in detail through each possible position on the cube, we will just highlight the key points around each:

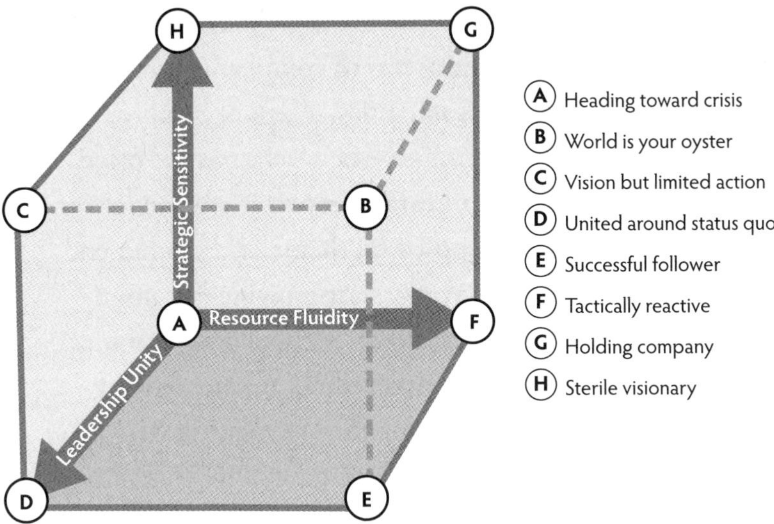

Figure 10.4: Strategic Options Based on Vectors of Strategic Agility

A—*Heading toward crisis.* At this extreme, companies are very weak and have little hope that growth or repositioning can be salvaged.

B—*World is your oyster.* This position denotes a high level of strategic agility that, conditional on a positive assessment of strategic assets and liabilities (as discussed in chapter 9), provides for a rich range of strategic options. The firm is agile. It can act with strength and determination and with strong strategic foresight, making commitments others would see as exceedingly risky.

C—*Vision but limited action.* Strong strategic sensitivity combined with leadership unity but with limited access to resources may enable one to take an early position in a new business, but it probably will not allow a company to sustain its growth or survive in the face of entry by fast followers. Unless, of course, alliances can provide access to complementary resources. In mature companies, a lack of resource fluidity is not uncommon—new ventures are often underfunded, and unrealistic expectations for "becoming big, fast" are imposed on them. At the other end of the spectrum are young, fast-growing but poorly funded innovative firms that, without access to complementary assets in market reach, manufacturing scale, brand equity, or even management skills, find themselves gobbled up by leading incumbents. From software developers to medical device manufacturers, the pattern is all too familiar. Being visionary and united is not enough—money and resources matter.

D—*United around status quo.* In general, strong positions on a single axis are the most precarious, and here, the somewhat paradoxical state of strong management unity but a lack of resource fluidity and strategic sensitivity makes for lame ducks. It is likely the executive team and the board are power- and position-oriented rather than results-oriented; they are perhaps stuck in the past or in a long-standing truce.

E—*Successful follower.* Leadership unity and resource fluidity combined make for successful followers. These "second entrants," in strategy jargon, succeed where the first movers may have lacked the necessary assets and resources. They are able to rapidly learn from the experience of the first movers and use that knowledge to develop stronger business models.

F—*Tactically reactive.* Another strong position on a single axis, a company with only a high degree of resource fluidity will be tactically but not strategically driven—moving resources around in reaction to immediate opportunities and dangers. Without strategic sensitivity or leadership unity, this constant knee-jerk reaction will undermine the long-term sustainability of the company.

G—*Holding company.* Strategic sensitivity and resource fluidity result in a strange situation in which executives are able to anticipate the market and have the resources available, but a lack of leadership unity leaves them failing to articulate and agree on a strategy.

H—*Sterile visionary.* Armed with only strategic sensitivity, we end up with sterile visionaries who are able to recognize what the future may look like but are unable to realize any vision.

The dialogue arising from plotting a company's position on the cube need not only be about the strategic options a company has. These positions are dynamic—they can easily deteriorate, or with focused intervention, they can improve. And so being aware of any deficits in strategic sensitivity, leadership unity, or resource allocation gives boards the opportunity to guide and work with senior management in turning these situations around and building a much more agile company that is able to adjust and adapt to a changing environment and avoid becoming victim of the growth curse. Take IBM, for instance. When Ginni Rometty took over as CEO in 2011, she inherited a firm in serious trouble. The three core businesses of hardware, high-margin software, and high-margin services were all in decline because clients were migrating to the cloud and IBM had no response. A Gartner survey of cloud infrastructure providers in August 2013 ranked IBM at the bottom of the 15 firms it studied.[2] In terms of innovation, apart from Watson (IBM's machine learning platform, which was not commercialized at the time), IBM had little to show for its $6 billion annual research and development budget. Clearly, it had lost its strategic sensitivity.

Leadership unity was in no better state, having been severely dented over the previous six years as a result of Sam Palmisano's (Rometty's predecessor) "roadmaps" policy to double earnings per share every five years. This pitted manager against manager and business against business, as IBM became first and foremost about meeting numbers. With 13 layers of management hierarchy all fighting to survive, competition was more prevalent than collaboration. The relentless pursuit of keeping shareholders happy also impacted resource allocation. On the one hand, resources were tightly controlled by the three core businesses, which by this time had become impenetrable silos. On the other hand, fierce cost cutting and arbitrage (particularly the shift of technical and engineering jobs from the United States to India) had left IBM with a skills and capabilities shortfall, so there simply weren't the people resources to allocate. Not surprisingly, morale hit rock bottom.

By the time Rometty stepped down as CEO in 2020, IBM had been transformed on all three vectors of strategic agility. Working closely with IBM's board, Rometty and her executive team had increased leadership unity by encouraging open and honest dialogue, creating a sense of being part of a team, and achieving collective commitment to IBM's goals and ambitions. Resource fluidity became an essential lever in Rometty's strategy to move away from the declining core businesses and refocus on big data and artificial intelligence (AI), mobile and social media technologies, and the cloud. Investments were made in both organic and acquisition-growth areas after a decade of being starved of funds. And as a result, staff were once again proud and excited to be working at IBM. Finally, if IBM were to compete against the likes of Google and Amazon, then strategic sensitivity had to become an ongoing and critical capability. Acquisitions such as SoftLayer and Red Hat brought new perspectives and insight into IBM (it's worth noting that Jim Whitehurst, the CEO of Red Hat, became the president of IBM) while partnerships with companies like Apple also increased IBM's strategic sensitivity. And its new customers in the domains of AI and the cloud also helped IBM envision how the future might look.

IBM achieved this shift to being more strategically agile and therefore having greater strategic options for the future in less than 10 years. And while there were initially rumblings of shareholder discontent (to be expected after the regime of managing a "successful" bottom line), the board openly supported Rometty and helped shareholders see the benefits of the transformation. For companies not facing a crisis and with weakness in just one or even two of the vectors, the path to regaining agility could be much shorter.

From Strategic Options to Avenues for Renewal

Thinking about strategic options in less abstract and more concrete terms, there are a number of different paths open for the board to explore depending on the firm's position on the cube. The most extreme profiles are the simplest and starkest. A firm already showing signs of decline and weak on all three vectors may not be worth attempting to save. Even if it still has strong strategic assets, such as a grand old brand or scarce and valuable real estate, for example, the board may decide that a new CEO and executive team would find it too difficult to rescue. And so, selling the assets may be the only realistic recourse. Some strategic assemblers will gladly buy them. For instance, consider how LVMH, the major French luxury goods and spirits company, has acquired a series of well-regarded but under-leveraged fashion and perfume brands, integrated them, and brought modern and effective marketing and operations management to them.

If a company is middling on most vectors or weak in only one and has strong strategic assets, rekindled growth is the way to go. But perhaps not in the way large companies have traditionally approached growth—where the emphasis has been on looking for major renewal options. As we explained in chapter 1, significant new growth opportunities are very difficult to find, particularly for large companies that have dominated markets for many years. Unless the company is in crisis and management has its collective back against the wall, the actions needed—redirecting resources from the core business to growth initiatives, building new systems and processes to fit those initiatives, hiring new people with the skills required for those initiatives, and taking a hit in the markets by admitting the core business is in terminal decline—are likely to be deemed too great a risk.

Given the difficulties and impediments to finding new big growth opportunities, a much more realistic and the only sustainable approach to growth is a continuous quest for smaller opportunities—a succession of micro "S-curves" and adjacencies—some of which may even score big eventually. Naturally, S-curves result in both periods of growth and times when growth flattens out. But when the board is armed with its strategic direction and has a good strategic dialogue with the CEO and executive team, these differences can be managed by ensuring there is always a pipeline of renewal (so that as some S-curves are petering out, others are entering the growth phase).

Growth at 3M, for instance, has come from micro S-curves for decades. The company was never chasing the next big thing but many small things its customers wanted. 3M was able to do this because it placed a high premium on innovation, with failures being seen as providing a critical knowledge bank for future growth; the culture was entrepreneurial; management let technical staff "do their thing"; and internal collaboration was not only encouraged but vital in allowing technologies to be linked across businesses, borrowed, and bootlegged to create new products.

Provided a company can count partnering among its strategic assets (or can actively build this capability), S-curve growth and renewal opportunities do not have to be limited to relying on the mobilization of existing internal resources. They can come from attracting complementary resources through alliances. Essilor, a world leader in ophthalmic optics, provides a case in point. Long-term partnerships are a core part of Essilor's growth strategy. Partnerships allow the company to enter new markets and new areas of activity very rapidly and over time support innovation by combining capabilities. For instance, Essilor entered the photochromic lens market in 1989 through an alliance with PPG, creating the Transitions brand. Combining Essilor's optical know-how and PPG's skills in chemicals and coatings led to Transitions rapidly becoming one of the leading brands in the market (in 2014, Essilor acquired PPG's stake in Transitions). An alliance with Nikon was initiated in 2000 to focus on market access. Over time, though, the two companies began joint innovation in new-generation materials, coatings, and more recently, the emerging fields of optoelectronics, precision optics, and advanced materials. Clearly, if a company can build the necessary skills for partnering, alliances can prove a very effective vehicle for steady growth and continual renewal.

Targeted acquisitions to access critical new capabilities, customers, or markets can provide a springboard to renewal, but only if their logic and rationale are clearly communicated throughout the company and their post-merger integration is handled with the utmost care and sensitivity—otherwise the risk of destroying value is increased. To avoid acquisitions becoming nothing but costly diversions, it would make sense to have made progress on improving resource fluidity and leadership unity if either of these vectors are weak beforehand (as Ginni Rometty did at IBM). It makes little sense to acquire a highly promising company only to starve it of resources or watch its management's entrepreneurial spirit wither in the face of your own dysfunctional and combative management practices.

The final avenue for renewal is to redeploy existing resources and competencies to pursue new options organically. Recall from chapter 9 how Fujifilm's CEO Shigetaka Komori undertook an inventory of the firm's technology to identify new areas for growth and refocus Fujifilm away from its high-margin core film business. This approach requires a bold decision by the board and CEO to purposefully shrink the business and risk the company's resources in a series of smaller new businesses that may or may not flourish. But if the company is in a declining industry and has some strong strategic assets, this approach of making multiple bets to find new S-curves to transform the company could make sense.

■

The headline message of this chapter is that to play an effective role in protecting the future of a firm, the board has to actively engage in assessing and understanding the strategic options available based on the extent of strategic sensitivity, leadership unity, and resource fluidity in the company. Sometimes, painful decisions have to be made, and there will be difficult conversations with shareholders whose expectations may not be aligned with the reality of the options on the table. But this process will strengthen the board's strategic dialogue with the CEO, lead to realistic and sustainable renewal, and stave off the risk of the company falling victim to the growth curse.

11 ■ Revitalizing the Company for Renewal

Even when armed with robust strategic options and a long-term strategic direction, a firm's renewal and transformation efforts can easily be thwarted at the implementation stage if a lack of energy and commitment runs through the company. We have already seen some of the ways in which culture is negatively affected when operationally focused mature companies have been through the wringer of the growth curse, resulting in a lack of leadership unity, infighting, political point scoring, misrepresentation, and a sense of despondency infecting the company at every level.

But even in companies that aren't consumed by the short-termism of managing the bottom line of a dominant core business, attempts to reenergize the strategy can still be undermined by a poor culture. The geographic and structural isolation of boards and the executive means that often those at the top are blissfully unaware of the significant cultural problems that can derail any renewal programs. A few years ago, the board of a fast-growing global firm asked us to assess whether the company had the structures and capabilities needed to expand into new strategic domains. As part of the project, we conducted a survey of staff from different locations around the world, different functions, and varying levels of seniority seeking to understand whether the company was culturally primed with the high levels of energy and commitment that would be essential for the ambitious strategy plans.

As we gathered in the conference room of a Paris hotel to reveal our findings, the board, CEO, and executive team were confident we would confirm their belief that the company had the strong and collaborative culture needed for the next growth phase. And to an extent they were right. We had found high levels of trust, collective commitment, collaboration, pride, motivation, purpose, and shared vision. Unfortunately, these attributes were limited to the operations in the company's small home country. And a consistently different picture emerged from everywhere else, where staff felt excluded from the home country cliques. They felt their ideas were never listened to and that they were second-class citizens on the periphery. They had no autonomy and saw the management structure as one of power and control flowing from the home country. They were unaware of any vision or sense of purpose the company had beyond what they saw as empty statements. With little intrinsic motivation, staff members were demotivated, and attrition rates were relatively high. We wrapped up the presentation of our findings to stunned silence from around the table as it had become clear that the culture outside the home country was in fact an obstacle to the successful implementation of the strategic ambition.

In firms today, achieving high levels of energy and commitment, particularly in large companies, is more difficult than ever, thanks to new disruptions, new technologies, emerging trends, and demographic changes. Individually, the challenges each of these issues poses is fairly obvious, but combined, the problem is of a much greater magnitude:

COVID pandemic and changing working practices—Before the COVID-19 pandemic swept its way around the world in 2020, few people could have imagined such a radical change to their daily work practices. Yet, as country after country went into lockdown, millions of people around the world suddenly found themselves working from home, and many chose to relocate out of crowded cities to more bucolic surroundings. And without the constant distractions of office life, productivity per hour worked increased by almost 5 percent in 2020—double the average annual growth rate of 2.4 percent.[1] For many, working from home was a positive change. It meant less micromanagement, more autonomy and freedom, no tiring commutes, and a better work-life balance with more time to spend with family and friends or pursuing personal interests.

Once the genie was out of the bottle, many people working from home became reluctant to return to office-based life full-time. And more people than ever are resigning from full-time employment to pursue other activities—a trend that had been increasing steadily until the "great resignation" in 2021.[2] In terms of culture, these trends provoke a number of questions: How do you motivate people to collaborate around a shared purpose when they are less and less colocated? Can you balance greater work flexibility with the personal and group interactions and processes needed for successful outcomes? How can you ensure certain functions or people are not excluded when flexible working is adopted? To keep people motivated and engaged, and to stem the trend of resignations, will incentives have to change? And with large numbers of people in their fifties retiring early, how do you fill the organizational knowledge and culture gaps left by these people—as many will be the upper middle and senior managers as well as mentors vital for driving energy and commitment?

Automation, AI, and de-skilling—Just as a combination of offshoring and robotic automation has had a significant impact on traditional manufacturing jobs in developed economies since the early 1990s and resulted in millions of workers losing their livelihoods, we are now witnessing the beginnings of a potentially seismic shift in the nature of many service-based and white-collar jobs, thanks to advances in artificial intelligence (AI) applications. The introduction of automation and AI leads to the de-skilling of many roles and leaves even less room for creativity, initiative, and decision-making—just think about the changing role of bank branch managers who not that long ago made loan decisions based on their knowledge of individual customers and today are delegated to trying to explain to customers why the algorithm has denied their application. Motivating and ensuring a sense of purpose for employees who are less and less empowered is going to be a big challenge for many large companies over the coming decades.

Growing inequality and loss of jobs for life—There was once a time when on joining a company out of school or university, there was every expectation that a lifelong career could be built there. And this was mutually beneficial because the futures of both employer and employee were closely intertwined—as an employee you were protected economically by lifetime employment, and for the company, there was pride and commitment from its staff. But the loss of a job for life, together with growing inequality in most societies, has led to anger and a sense of disenfranchisement for many middle-income and lower-income workers, destroying the balance of that relationship. If employees don't see their labor resulting in increased income, wealth, and quality of life improvements and instead feel they are being exploited rather than valued (particularly in light of growing pay gaps between average employees and senior executives), the task of infusing a company with energy and commitment will be an uphill battle because commitment is a two-way street.

Millennials and Generation Z—We have already touched on the differing attitudes of millennials and Generation Z in chapter 2, with regard to how they believe companies should protect rather than destroy the environment. And in general, they also have a very different perspective on the nature of work: They want to do something meaningful that has an impact, and they are much less inclined to start at the bottom of a large company and work their way up to a position in which they can make a difference. Like many business schools, INSEAD has seen this shift firsthand—where for decades, prestigious investment banks and large global companies could have their pick of MBA graduates, in the last 15 years, the best and brightest MBA students have been turning their backs on these traditional recruiters in favor of start-ups and more exciting agile, entrepreneurial firms where they can have a voice and have an impact.

These generations also place a greater value on work-life balance and are less inclined to remain in one firm for a long time—switching jobs and companies to meet their personal objectives in life and skills-accumulation needs. Clearly, attracting, motivating, energizing, stimulating, and gaining commitment and loyalty from a workforce with a much more fluid attitude to jobs and a desire to do good and make a difference will pose a growing challenge, particularly for mature large companies.

People really do matter for the long-term, sustainable success of a company. But the confluence of the four trends we have outlined presents a significant added hurdle to building a durable, positive culture. Employees and potential employees are now likely to be less committed and less motivated to work for firms that don't offer them the flexibility, autonomy, rewards, or sense of meaning and purpose that are increasingly important.

With concerns about the impact of these emerging trends in mind but focusing primarily on the present, it is imperative for the board (as well as the CEO and executive team) to understand whether there is enough energy, commitment, and motivation throughout the firm to drive strategy forward or whether a culture of inertia and despondency will likely kill any strategic initiative. Over the following pages, we are going to outline some of the behaviors and factors common in low-energy cultures, suggest some starting points for assessing firm culture, and finally discuss what is needed to rekindle a culture of energy and commitment crucial for continual strategic renewal.

Indicators of Low-Energy, Low-Commitment Cultures

Although dysfunctional low-energy cultures are a feature of growth curse firms, as we touched on earlier, they can permeate any company and are rarely obvious to those at the very top of those companies. To help boards recognize the symptoms of an unhealthy culture, we have identified five broad categories in which weaknesses can be easily recognized: purpose, management style, commitment, emotional climate, and job satisfaction.

Lack of Purpose

Weak cultures will favor an excessive operational focus over a compelling sense of purpose. As we discussed in detail in chapter 7 (when looking at the failure of the strategy process), an internal operational focus aimed at achieving efficiencies to drive short-term bottom-line growth naturally results in a lack of investment in people and facilities, which in turn leads to staff feeling dissatisfied and undervalued. The ever more unrealistic performance targets imposed by an operational focus bring stress and tension and give rise to infighting between teams and divisions. As pressure mounts, misrepresentation is often resorted to as the only way for individuals and teams to meet performance expectations.

Top-Down Management

Bottom-up initiatives are a sign that staff are engaged and feel empowered to contribute to the company's future. When they start to dwindle and disappear in favor of top-down diktats, this is a red flag that there will be growing dissatisfaction among the ranks. A top-down management approach disenfranchises staff members. They lose confidence in their judgment and skills and shy away from challenges that they believe they may fail in. A general feeling of negativity pervades the culture, which makes any turnaround extremely difficult.

In addition, the strengthening of hierarchical command-and-control structures and systems imposes a culture of compliance in the worst meaning of the term. Staff have no autonomy or freedom and see themselves only as part of a production line, performing a specific role rather than contributing to the vibrancy and future success of the company. Compliance usually comes with reams of policies and procedures to be followed; as employees begin to feel even less valued and less trusted, their energy and commitment will decline. And nowhere is this felt more than in the layers of middle management, where extreme frustration grows at being reduced to merely serving as the conduit for executive and senior management's latest plans.

Lack of Commitment

Changing expectations of working practices, de-skilling, growing inequality, and demographic changes are already putting a strain on employee commitment to the firms they work for. The situation is much worse in firms with poor or toxic cultures. Here, in place of a sense of one company with everyone pulling in the same ultimate direction, cliques begin to form, with people rallying around individuals with competing views. Choices are then made based more on interpersonal likes and dislikes and loyalty to an individual, not the business or the company. Open and honest dialogue is replaced with politicized point scoring, and it becomes difficult for staff to stand on the sidelines because to survive, everyone needs to belong to a tribe.

When companies have fragmented organizational structures, conflictual relationships, and dysfunctional communication, the likelihood of collaboration taking place becomes even more remote. When lines of accountability are fuzzy and there is no sense of integration across the company, the need to commit to a particular tribe will be even stronger, to the detriment of a cohesive culture.

Negative Emotional Climate

A sense of frustration and negative emotions color how staff feel about their work and the organization. As more demands are heaped on employees in conjunction with greater constraints, less freedom, and less autonomy, it's common for pride, loyalty, and a sense of purpose to be replaced by lethargy, resentment, fear, and tension. Look at any company teetering on the edge of decline and there is a common pattern of energy being directed toward infighting between teams and divisions. To paraphrase a common saying, "With energy and commitment like that, who needs competitors?"

Once the energy and commitment in a company have deteriorated to the level of obvious internal hostilities and a total reluctance to question decisions or reveal inconvenient or uncomfortable truths, the toxic culture in the company will be palpable.

Poor Job Satisfaction

People deriving low levels of job satisfaction from the work they do is clear sign of a lack of energy and commitment. This often comes about because staff begin to feel frustrated. There is little appreciation for what they do, even though more and more is expected of them. We have seen time and time again how after rounds of deep job cuts, employees can end up doing what the previous year had been the jobs of two, three, or even four people, with neither thanks nor additional resources to support them (but always with the sword of Damocles hanging over them that "next time it could be your job to go"). Pushed beyond the limits of what is emotionally, mentally, cognitively, and physically possible, this leads to burnout.

It's not just overwork that leads to low levels of job satisfaction. Even the most committed people can quickly become demotivated if they don't find their work meaningful or if they come up against barriers that prevent them from doing a good job. Research into the psychological impact of barriers to performance on the 75th US Ranger Regiment deployed to Somalia in the early 1990s found that although the soldiers were highly motivated on arrival, uncertainty about their role and a constantly shifting mission prevented them from doing their jobs and lowered morale. In fact, those who cared most about their work were even more demoralized and demotivated because they were unable to succeed and do something they believed was important.[3]

The loss of employment for life, changes to working practices hastened by the pandemic, and the different attitudes of younger generations all mean people feel less bound to the companies they work for, and when people are unhappy or unsatisfied at work, they are more likely to resign. So, low levels of job satisfaction will be seen in higher attrition rates. At first, the best and brightest talent will leave, but over time, higher attrition will be seen across the firm. And the time new hires stay with the company will also decrease. And let's not forget that with social media and websites rating employers, dissatisfied employees have plenty of channels to share their thoughts and experience.

Assessing Energy and Commitment in a Firm

Understanding the roots of the dominant logic of a company—in other words, what underpins the cultural norms and beliefs—is a good first step in assessing culture. Past successes become codified in a dominant logic and often remain unchallenged, even when they are no longer relevant to the emerging competitive landscape. So arraying the constituents of the dominant logic against the company's strategic options and long-term strategic direction will highlight which beliefs and practices should be preserved, which should be discarded, and which need to be changed. The distance between where the company stands today in terms of culture and where it needs to be for renewal to be successful will become clear at a high, broad-brush level.

For a more detailed assessment, specialist consultants have a range of tools and methods to evaluate the state of a firm's culture. In firms displaying all the five indicators of a lack of energy and commitment (no sense of purpose, top-down management, low levels of commitment, negative emotional climate, and poor job satisfaction), it makes sense to bring in outside experts to help. Fearful staff will be much more likely to give an honest assessment of how they feel and how they perceive the company to an outsider rather than participate in an internal audit of culture. For example, concern about reprisals may prevent people from opening up, and staff may not trust employee opinion surveys, even if they are administered anonymously, and so they won't give honest feedback.

It is important that any assessment of culture isn't seen as just another initiative imposed by the board or executive team. Patrick Butler, an expert on culture with a focus on highly regulated industries, told us, "For change to take hold, the process needs to be collectively owned from the outset as the outcome of a culture assessment has to lead to action. I often start with a real-time culture snapshot," he said, "where staff are asked to rate the importance of a range of behavioral competencies and then asked the extent to which each of these are observed in their organization. This instantly reveals gaps in culture and is powerful in capturing everyone's interest, from the most senior to most junior. Once we have widespread attention and engagement, we can then do a more granular deep dive."[4]

What a deep-dive assessment of culture involves will vary by company, but it should certainly aim to investigate the underlying problems within each of the five indicators of low-energy and low-commitment cultures. Starting with "purpose," many firms have their mission or purpose emblazoned on their websites, but a few relatively straightforward questions can quickly reveal whether these statements are genuinely embedded in the culture or are simply window dressing in an operationally focused company. Let's take an example we know of: A survey of more than 100 senior and middle managers at a troubled European bank revealed all of them knew only one of the firm's purported values, and this happened to be the one that had been the subject of an internal communication the previous week.

The fact that the values were "on the company intranet" but not known, understood, or embraced by staff showed they were meaningless and not a core driver of energy and commitment.

From the processes and systems in place, the management style of a company should be obvious—although it isn't always clear-cut because there is a lot of space on the spectrum between the extremes of hierarchical power and control approaches and the autonomy of self-managing teams. To gauge the extent to which bottom-up initiatives are encouraged and freedom valued, it is best to probe middle management, with the following questions as a starting point:

What do they see as the characteristics that define a "good manager" in the firm? What skills are valued? What are the personal characteristics needed for a manager to succeed (is it purely about meeting financial targets, or are initiative, motivational skills, collaboration, communication, and commitment rewarded)?

Do they focus on the status quo or change?

Do senior managers provide general rules for decision-making? How are disagreements raised and resolved?

Do they feel management systems (such as budgeting, planning, compensation, and career progression) are consistent in supporting the strategic goals of line managers? What are the barriers to success in achieving goals? What constraints do middle managers face?

Do they communicate regularly and informally with colleagues (including those in different functions and business units) to work on common problems and solutions, or is communication usually through formal meetings involving senior oversight?

The answers to these questions will be revealing in understanding where management decisions are concentrated. They will also provide insight into how valued, happy, and committed middle managers feel, and this knowledge can be taken as a proxy for the culture of the company as a whole.

Rekindling Energy and Commitment

Any change in culture takes time and will only be successful if the board and the executive team remain committed to the change for long enough for new behaviors, processes, systems, and relationships to take root within the firm. To get everyone in the company on board, it's not only vital that messaging is clear and consistent but that changes in behavior can be easily observed in those at the top. And in companies where morale and energy are low, this will require a change in leadership to someone bringing new energy, drive, and attitudes that can reignite excitement, a sense of purpose, and commitment of staff throughout the firm.

This is exactly what happened at Microsoft. In the decade leading up to 2014, despite increased profits, Microsoft had lost its way. Gone was its ability to innovate, growth was flat, and its culture had become toxic. Its infamous stack ranking performance appraisal system meant that in every team, some people would score poorly regardless of the contribution they had made. This killed collaboration, encouraged internal competition, and led to a culture of backbiting where everyone was out to protect themselves. Talented engineers left in droves.

In 2014, long-time Microsoft insider Satya Nadella was selected to replace Steve Ballmer as CEO. With a very different background, personality, and management style than his predecessor, the reflective Nadella believed in Microsoft's ability to be a great innovative growth company again, but he knew changing the culture would be key to this transformation. Nadella emphasized the importance of empathy, collaboration, and continual learning for everyone in Microsoft. The stack ranking review system was abolished, a new executive team was established, openness and honesty were practiced as well as preached, listening to and learning from customers and colleagues was encouraged, and a shift to growth mindsets in the firm began. With new energy and commitment throughout the company, Microsoft was transformed into a fast-growing tech firm with strong new businesses in AI and cloud computing to complement its Windows, Office, and gaming businesses.

Returning to our five broad categories on which the state of a company's culture can be viewed, figure 11.1 illustrates the stark differences between companies suffering from burnout and decline and those exhibiting high energy and high commitment. And here it's worth remembering the research of Charles O'Reilly and Jeff Pfeffer, who found that the best-performing companies weren't those full of extraordinary people; rather, they were companies with cultures that brought out the best in ordinary people.[5] So what does it take to create an extraordinary culture and shift from being a low-energy to a high-energy firm?

Purpose—It Has to Be Compelling
Rebuilding energy and commitment requires staff to be focused on a compelling and meaningful purpose, together with clear

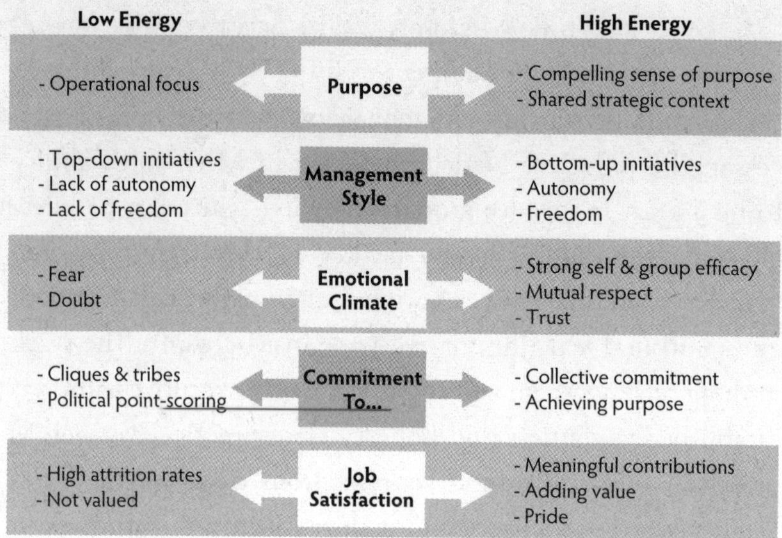

Figure 11.1: Characteristics of High- and Low-Energy Firms

goals. We would argue this journey will be made easier if the board has defined a strategic direction, has agreed on clear strategic options with the CEO, and this strategic thinking has been shared, explained, and discussed throughout the company. And this is an important thing that shouldn't be overlooked: Ask yourself, how many of the employees in your company understand the company's strategy? Ask what your aims are and how you are going to get there. You may find surprisingly few people really understand what it is they are contributing to, day-in and day-out.

Some years back, we were asked to help a global industrial company work out why some of its large global innovation projects succeeded and others failed. One of the critical factors we found was the extent to which the strategic context of the project had or hadn't been explained and understood. When teams knew the strategic purpose of the project, they collaborated and worked toward the same goal; they were able to rapidly find good solutions to problems they encountered and were much more engaged, creative, and motivated to deliver the project on time. They had energy and were committed. When the strategic rationale was lacking, competing visions derailed or delayed projects. There was less team cohesion, key staff left mid-project, problems tended to result in stalemates, and employees didn't recognize the true value or purpose of what they were doing. People became disillusioned and fed up.

Of course, as well as a compelling sense of purpose and clear goals, employee focus can also be directed to threats. Andy Grove explained how "paranoia" helped Intel recognize and overcome strategic inflection points.[6] However, in companies that have been stuck in the growth curse, when levels of engagement are already fragile and employees are suffering from low morale, low energy, and low motivation, getting them energized around a more positive focus—the ambition of the new strategy—might be a more effective approach than trying to rally them around fear.

Management—Give People Freedom

A shift from a top-down management approach has to start with the process of culture change itself. It is important to emphasize that culture change is not something that can be "imposed" from the top. Middle management has to drive the effort. These managers are connected to much greater networks of staff and have a better understanding of the pulse of a company. Most will readily champion a culture that allows them to exercise choice and take control of their time instead of saying "yes" to everyone and constantly juggling fragmented schedules.

Because autonomy and freedom are needed for successful bottom-up initiatives, a number of changes will be needed in management processes, systems, and approaches. The emphasis on planning has to be replaced by a focus on adaptation, flexibility, and learning. The role of senior managers should change from decision maker to "sense maker," process designer, and facilitator. And a common language and decision processes have to be adopted across the firm to build trust and support lateral collaboration.

Empowerment shouldn't stop with middle management. Teams will be more creative and engaged if individual team members are given responsibility and autonomy and are involved in decision-making. Contrary to what one might expect, research has shown that delegating autonomy to individuals does not come at the expense of the effective functioning of teams or larger groups.[7] It is simply not the case that freedom and autonomy will result in "too many cooks." It is more likely that they lead to pride in the work being done, a sense of purpose about goals, and a commitment to achieving those goals.

Commitment—Sharing a Sense of Purpose

Even without the type of dysfunctional tribalism that flourishes in rotten corporate cultures, a lot of commitment will remain localized. While people can believe in a strong and compelling broad purpose, on a day-to-day basis, the strongest sense of satisfaction and purpose will come from working within teams, functions, and business groups, and accordingly, this is where commitment will be strongest. So it is imperative that the right support, structures, and processes are in place to provide clarity and build the trust and mutual respect required for collective commitment throughout the firm.

Emotional Climate—Positive Energy

People will generally be more committed in positive emotional environments that focus on opportunities rather than obstacles. In positive environments, individuals can both contribute to and learn from interactions, different perspectives are valued, and there is a sense of progress as goals are achieved.[8] Identifying "energizers"—people whose own positive energy is contagious and who motivate the people around them—and seeding these people through the firm can really help elevate the emotional climate and energize a company.

A sense of energy can also come from confidence. In his seminal 1977 paper, Stanford University psychologist Albert Bandura described self-efficacy as a belief in one's own ability to succeed in a given situation.[9] This can stem from mastering a previous challenge, seeing colleagues and peers succeed in a specific task, or being encouraged to overcome self-doubt and persuaded that you have the skills to succeed.

Strong self-efficacy creates a positive feedback loop: The greater the belief people have that they can succeed, the greater their job satisfaction, motivation, and energy; consequently, they will be more likely to succeed—even when facing ambitious challenges. People with high levels of self-efficacy are problem solvers and recover quickly from setbacks. And the same holds true for group efficacy. Previous successes raise belief in the group's ability to succeed more generally. When everyone understands what each individual team member contributes, when there is a proven method for integrating those contributions, and when the team collectively recognizes value in what they have been tasked with, a team's belief in its ability can positively impact its performance and the sense of satisfaction of its members.[10]

Job Satisfaction—Meaningful Work

Beyond generating excitement with vision and goals, people need to be satisfied with their jobs and feel they are making meaningful contributions—both on a daily basis in the way they help their team achieve its goals and more generally in the way they feel there is value in what they and the company do. A clear strategy and strong sense of purpose to serve a wide range of stakeholders will offer staff both meaning and satisfaction in their work and in turn have a positive impact on the energy and commitment levels in the firm.

■

High-energy companies are characterized by high levels of freedom and autonomy, where people are given goals or missions and are also empowered with the flexibility to decide how best to reach them. Management that clings to power-control relationships, whether at the executive, business, or local team level, will never reignite the energy and commitment needed to drive the company's ambition. To escape the growth curse trap and revitalize a company so it can successfully navigate the challenges of renewal, management must impassion, engage, motivate, and instill a sense of pride and purpose in the company's employees.

Some Final Thoughts

Since we began the research leading to this book, the confluence of a number of unanticipated events have made the world
a much more fragile place: The COVID-19 pandemic had a
devastating effect not only on people's physical and mental
health, but it ushered in the largest global economic crisis in
living memory and some of the highest levels of public and private debt since the end of World War II. And in another first,
Russia's invasion of Ukraine in early 2022 marked the first major war on European soil in over 70 years. This led to global
food supply disruption (Ukraine is the world's largest supplier
of sunflower oil and, along with Russia, one of the biggest grain
exporters), and it deepened the energy crisis that had already

begun post-pandemic (Russia is the world's second-largest supplier of natural gas).

Global inflation shot up to 8.8 percent in 2022 from around 3.5 percent in the pre-pandemic 2017–2019 period.[1] Central banks around the world rapidly increased interest rates, and millions of hard-pressed families in the developed world found themselves plunged into poverty. In early 2023, vulnerabilities from excessive debt in the financial system, which had been rumbling in the background for some time, came to the fore with the collapse of Silicon Valley Bank and Signature Bank in the United States, followed by the fall of the venerable Swiss global banking giant Credit Suisse.

The delicate equilibrium between the world's superpowers also began to come under strain as fractures along geopolitical lines took hold—something that hasn't been helped by the beginnings of a retreat from globalization brought about in some cases by sanctions and in others by the realization that supply chains need to be more resilient.

Although not a new problem—Plato, Hobbes, and perhaps most famously Rousseau all wrote of the dangers of wealth and social inequality for the fabric of society as a whole—growing inequality of wealth and consequently opportunity within and between nations became an increasing concern, exacerbated by the fact that for the first time in decades there is widespread doubt about the future of employment. And with record levels of mass migration across the Mediterranean and Rio Grande, populist political movements were quick to seize on and exploit the fears of ordinary people, further damaging societal cohesion.

Yet the impact of these unanticipated events are perhaps all overshadowed by the multifaceted tragedy of environmental crisis and climate change. According to estimates from the

World Health Organization (WHO), air pollution is responsible for the deaths of up to 7 million people a year.[2] The loss of biodiversity, caused by the deforestation taking place to make way for farming, mining, and oil and gas production, is increasing. So is the chronic pollution of our oceans. While human activity is pushing many species closer to extinction, there is hope that the damage is not completely irreversible. *The Year the Earth Changed*, a documentary film made by the BBC Natural History Unit, showed how the lockdowns and travel restrictions in 2020 allowed many species to flourish that year.[3]

Long an issue in sub-Saharan Africa, the impact of water shortages from climate change is now being felt more widely across the globe. And not only does climate change cost nation-states billions of dollars annually, resulting directly from extreme weather events, but it is leading to poorer crop yields and food shortages.

In 2022, the 17th edition of the *World Economic Forum Global Risks Report* identified five of the eight most severe global risks over the next 10 years as being environment issues, with climate action failure, extreme weather events, and loss of biodiversity ranking as the top-three threats.[4] These environmental challenges are amplified when taken in conjunction with a growing world population, which is forecast to increase by more than 25 percent by 2050.[5] Taking all these problems into consideration (the consequences of unanticipated events and environmental damage), it seems clear that the world is becoming a more uncertain and precarious place.

In case you are now afraid that we are reciting a depressingly modern-day version of the Plagues of Egypt (only the locusts are missing!), let us reassure you. The Chinese character for crisis means "danger and opportunity," and this is true of the current situation, too. Clearly, the COVID pandemic exacted a terrible toll in human life and disrupted our economies and our lives, but it also spurred mRNA research at Pfizer-BioNTech and Moderna, opening avenues for treating many other diseases, including cancer.

Of course, as we write, the war in Ukraine is still killing innocent people every day and disturbing our economies, but the need to wean us off Russian gas has accelerated the development of renewable energies and created huge growth areas. Climate change has triggered lots of extreme weather events, devastating droughts and floods, tornados and hurricanes, but the need to find alternatives to fossil fuel use has opened up new opportunities—driving innovation in a wide range of industries, from automobiles to energy, with nuclear fusion, which seemed like a sci-fi dream just a few years ago, now promising the possibility of unbound clean energy in our lifetimes.

After having contributed to many of the problems we are facing today while at the same time benefiting from liberal capitalism for decades, corporations need to change. And some are already being strategic in identifying and seizing opportunities to be part of the solution. They are spearheading new technologies, systems, and approaches that not only give them competitive advantage but also address some of the world's critical challenges. But more businesses have to become a force for good, for people, for the planet, and for our future.

Of course, economics teaches us that the search for profits and the value they create already provide a formidable force for good. Profits make growth and vital innovation possible. From that viewpoint, the "business of business is business," with the implication that company leaders should avoid themselves or the organizations they lead being drawn into social and political activism. Yet, most of the fundamental challenges we face cannot be successfully addressed by democratically elected governments alone; they require wider collaboration with a variety of stakeholders, companies included.

Business leaders have to become more sensitive to the longer-term impact of their actions, and like it or not, they have to apply additional criteria to that of creating shareholder wealth in measuring their success. However, our research found that corporate leaders are often hesitant and uncertain about assuming a wider mantle, and many of them are woefully unprepared to do so. They need to raise their sights and up their game from achieving operational performance in their firms to contributing to solve the societal challenges of the economic and social system they are part of. And that calls for them to turn their backs on the lamentable practice of short-termism and learn to work with multiple stakeholders in handling complexity and the unanticipated problems and strategic surprises that complexity brings. But clearly, CEOs can't do this alone.

One of the starting motivations for writing this book was our observation that in facing these growing challenges, governance and strategic management have remained very separate areas. Throughout this book we have shown why and how this gap needs to be bridged. In the wider, more complex, and more demanding context that companies now face, boards have to play a stronger role. They have to provide a beacon, a guiding light offering a sense of direction anchored in a long-term ambition and serving a worthwhile purpose. Boards need to be future-oriented, not auditors of the past. Boards also need to become the guardians of ethics and honesty, shielding management from the most brutal short-term pressures that encourage management misbehavior.

Making governance more strategic is not just about ensuring companies are better managed; it's about making them better citizens of the world. It's a lever for building better societies, making the world a better place, and for protecting us against the greed unleashed by the folly of financialization and sometimes that of successful CEOs. Strategic governance will also alleviate the pressures that make the life of CEOs, their teams, and the many people who work for them miserable. Serving a long-term strategy with the support of the board and shareholders is certainly a better fate than facing the quarterly meat grinder of stock analysts and living in fear of corporate raiders. And companies that have a genuine purpose and make a positive impact through their actions will be better workplaces for everyone, not just the younger generations, who often believe that shareholder capitalism is responsible for many woes and who rightly prioritize safeguarding the future.

Chapter 1

1. United Nations Department of Economic and Social Affairs, Population Division, *World Population Prospects 2022: Summary of Results*, UN DESA/POP/2022/TR/NO. 3 (New York: United Nations, 2022).

2. United Nations Educational, Scientific and Cultural Organization, *Reading the Past, Writing the Future: Fifty Years of Promoting Literacy* (Paris: UNESCO, 2017); and World Bank, "Literacy Rate, Adult Total," accessed January 12, 2023, https://data.worldbank.org/indicator/SE.ADT.LITR.ZS.

3. Dominic Barton, James Manyika, Timothy Koller, Robert Palter, and Jonathan Godsall, "Measuring the Economic Impact of Short-Termism," McKinsey Global Institute Discussion Paper, February 2017.

4. Increasing returns to adoption is a very simple phenomenon. In stylized terms, the value of a good or service to a customer increases with how many other customers buy and use the same thing, thus conferring the supplier with a natural monopoly character. This becomes two-sided when both customers and suppliers benefit from interdependent and mutually growing returns to adoption. As an example, consider the codependency between stores subscribing to a credit card brand and network like Visa and the consumers who carry that particular credit card in their wallet.

5. Yves Doz and Keeley Wilson, *Ringtone: Exploring the Rise and Fall of Nokia in Mobile Phones* (Oxford: Oxford University Press, 2015).

6. Drake Bennett, "The Gore-Tex Eye," *Bloomberg BusinessWeek*, May 13, 2019.

Chapter 2

1. Michael C. Jensen and William H. Meckling, "Theory of the Firm: Managerial Behavior, Agency Costs and Ownership Structure," *Journal of Financial Economics* 3, no. 4 (October 1976): 305–360.

2. Business Roundtable, "Statement on Corporate Governance," white paper, September 1997, https://cdn.theconversation.com/static_files/files/693/Statement_on_Corporate_Governance_Business-Roundtable-1997(1).pdf.

3. Business Roundtable, "Our Commitment: Statement on the Purpose of a Corporation," August 19, 2019, https://opportunity.businessroundtable.org/ourcommitment/.

4. Harvard Law School Forum on Corporate Governance, "BRT Statement of Corporate Purpose: Debate Continues," August 28, 2020, https://corpgov.law.harvard.edu/2020/08/28/brt-statement-of-corporate-purpose-debate-continues/; Stephen M. Bainbridge, "Making Sense of the Business Roundtable's Reversal on Corporate Purpose," UCLA School of Law, Law-Econ Research Paper No. 20–03, *46 Journal of Corporation Law 285* (2021).

5. For a succinct and well-argued critique, see Joseph L. Bower and Lynn S. Paine, "The Error at the Heart of Corporate Leadership," *Harvard Business Review* (May–June 2017): 50–60.

6. "Lazard's Review of Shareholder Activism 2022," January 18, 2023, https://www.lazard.com/research-insights/lazard-s-review-of-shareholder-activism-2022.

7. Richard Milne, "Norwegian Oil Fund to Vote against Companies without Net Zero Targets," *Financial Times*, December 7, 2022, https://www.ft.com/content/d681cabf-3189-442c-a9ed-2fd51b2f68fd.

8. Lucian A. Bebchuk and Scott Hirst, "Big Three Power, and Why It Matters," *Boston University Law Review* 102 (December 2022): 1547–1600.

9. BlackRock's website has an archive of Larry Fink's letters to CEOs from 2012 to the present; see https://www.blackrock.com/corporate/investor-relations/larry-fink-ceo-letter.

10. Lucian A. Bebchuk and Scott Hirst, "Index Funds and the Future of Corporate Governance: Theory, Evidence, and Policy," *Columbia Law Review* 119 (December 2019): 2029–2146.

11. Mark R. Desjardine, "Under Pressure: The Causal Effect of Financial Analyst Coverage on Long-Term Capital Investments," *Academy of Management Proceedings* 2015, no. 1 (2015), https://doi.org/10.5465/AMBPP.2015.72.

12. Akrur Barua and Patricia Buckley, "Rising Corporate Debt: Should We Worry?" *Deloitte Insights Issues by the Numbers*, April 15, 2019, https://www2.deloitte.com/us/en/insights/economy/issues-by-the-numbers/rising-corporate-debt-levels.html.

13. Lawrence Mishel and Julia Wolfe, "CEO Compensation Has Grown 940% since 1978: Typical Worker Compensation Has Risen Only 12% during That Time," *Economic Policy Institute Report*, August 14, 2019, https://www.epi.org/publication/ceo-compensation-2018/.

14. Amit Batish, "Equilar: New York Times 200 Highest-Paid CEOs," *Equilar*, June 25, 2022, https://www.equilar.com/reports/95-equilar-new-york-times-top-200-highest-paid-ceos-2022.

15. High Pay Centre, "CEO Pay Survey 2022: CEO Pay Surges 39%," August 22, 2022, https://highpaycentre.org/ceo-pay-survey-2022-ceo-pay-surges-39/.

16. Eric Béziat, "Stellantis CEO Carlos Tavares' 66-Million-Euro Earnings Spark Outrage," *Le Monde*, April 14, 2022, https://www.lemonde.fr/en/economy/article/2022/04/14/stellantis-ceo-carlos-tavares-66-million-euro-earnings-spark-outrage_5980538_19.html.

17. The Limited Times, "14 Million Euros Annual Salary—This Is the Highest-Paid CEO in the Dax," July 14, 2021, https://newsrnd.com/news/2021-07-14-14-million-euros-annual-salary---this-is-the-highest-paid-ceo-in-the-dax.r1bbIrU36O.html.

18. "663 Executives of Listed Companies Earned More than ¥100 Million in FY21," *Japan News*, July 24, 2022, https://japannews.yomiuri.co.jp/business/companies/20220724-46717/.

19. "HCL Tech's C Vijayakumar Is One of the Highest-Paid Indian IT CEOs: Here's How Much He Earns," *Financial Express*, February 19, 2023, https://www.financialexpress.com/lifestyle/hcl-tech-ceo-c-vijayakumars-salary-is-more-than-mukesh-ambanis-2020-pay-check-his-earnings-and-net-worth/2985711/.

20. Patrick Durkin, "Revealed: Australia's 50 Highest-Paid CEOs in 2022," *Financial Review*, December 9, 2022, https://www.afr.com/work-and-careers/workplace/revealed-australia-s-50-highest-paid-ceos-in-2022-20221205-p5c306.

21. Michael J. Cooper, Huseyin Gulen, and P. Raghavendra Rau, "Performance for Pay? The Relation between CEO Incentive Compensation and Future Stock Price Performance," November 1, 2016, https://ssrn.com/abstract=1572085.

22. Yves Doz, Eeva Hellstrom, Mikko Kosonen, Jenna Lahdemaki, and Kelley Wilson, "Reflections on the 'Leadership under Complexity' Workshop," *SITRA Working Papers*, March 17, 2017, https://www.sitra.fi/en/publications/reflections-the-leadership-under-complexity-workshop/.

23. Nassim Nicholas Taleb, *The Black Swan: the Impact of the Highly Improbable* (New York: Random House, 2007).

24. Warren Weaver, "Science and Complexity," *American Scientist* 36, no. 4 (1948): 536–544; see also the latest edition by Ross Wirth, "Science and Complexity: Warren Weaver," *Emergence: Complexity & Organization* 6, no. 3 (2004): 65–74.

25. Weaver, "Science and Complexity."

26. Ikujiro Nonaka and Hirotaka Takeuchi, "The Wise Leader," *Harvard Business Review* 89, no. 5 (May 2011): 58–67.

Chapter 3

1. Ronald W. Clement, "Just How Unethical Is American Business?" *Business Horizons* 49, no. 4 (July–August 2006): 313–327.

2. Peter Fleming and Stelios C. Zyglidopoulos, "The Escalation of Deception in Organizations," *Journal of Business Ethics* 81 (2008): 837–850.

3. Gresham M. Sykes and David Matza, "Techniques of Neutralization: A Theory of Delinquency," *American Sociological Review* 22, no. 6 (1957): 664–670.

4. S&P Global, "S&P 500 Buybacks Set Quarterly and Annual Record," press release, March 15, 2022, https://press.spglobal.com/2022-03-15-S-P-500-Buybacks-Set-Quarterly-and-Annual-Record.

5. Jenal Mehta, "FTSE 100 Share Buybacks Double in 2022: Will These Bumper Pay-Outs Last?" *Capital.Com*, August 3, 2022, https://capital.com/ftse-100-share-buybacks-double-in-2022-will-these-bumper-pay-outs-last.

6. BNP Parisbas, "European Corporate Share Buyback Volumes Almost Doubled in 2022," February 13, 2023, https://globalmarkets.cib.bnpparibas/european-corporate-share-buyback-volumes-almost-doubled-in-2022/.

7. Jesse M. Fried and Charles C. Y. Wang, "Short-Termism and Capital Flows," *Review of Corporate Finance Studies* 8, no. 1 (March 2019): 207–233.

8. Shawn Tully, "Destruction of Capital: How GE's Decade of Stock Buybacks May Come Back to Haunt the Company," *Fortune*, August 22, 2019.

9. "General Electric Picks New Boss," *The Economist*, June 17, 2017.

10. Annet Aris, interview by authors July 2018.

11. Thomas Gryta, "GE Confronts Legacy of Bad Power Deals," *Wall Street Journal*, October 8, 2019.

12. Thomas Gryta, "GE Faces an SEC Probe of Accounts," *Wall Street Journal*, January 25, 2018.

13. US Securities and Exchange Commission, "SEC Charges General Electric with Accounting Fraud," press release 2009–178, August 4, 2009, https://www.sec.gov/news/press/2009/2009-178.htm.

14. Steve Johnson, "Retired 3M Chief Finds a New Life in Sustainability," *Financial Times*, January 20, 2013.

Chapter 4

1. Robert Armstrong, "Rising Tide of Lawsuits against Company Directors Hits Insurers," *Financial Times*, April 1, 2019; Clifford Chance, "The Rising Tide of Litigation against Directors," *The In-House Lawyer*, Autumn 2018, https://www.cliffordchance.com/content/dam/cliffordchance/PDFDocuments/ihl-au18-p30-33-advertorial-clifford-chance.pdf.

2. Daisuke Wakabayashi and Kate Conger, "Board Sued over Google's Exit Package for Accused Executive," *New York Times*, January 10, 2019.

3. Damian Carrington, "Shell Directors Personally Sued over 'Flawed' Climate Strategy," *The Guardian*, February 9, 2023, https://www.theguardian.com/environment/2023/feb/09/shell-directors-personally-sued-over-flawed-climate-strategy.

4. Risto Siilasmaa, *Transforming Nokia* (New York: McGraw-Hill, 2019).

5. Vasily Klucharev, Kaisa Hytönen, Mark Rijpkema, Ale Smidts, and Guillen Fernández, "Reinforcement Learning Signal Predicts Social Conformity," *Neuron* 61, no. 1 (2009): 140–151.

6. Gregory S. Berns, Jonathan Chappelow, Caroline F. Zink, Giuseppe Pagnoni, Megan E. Martin-Skurski, and Jim Richards, "Neurobiological Correlates of Social Conformity and Independence during Mental Rotation," *Biological Psychiatry* 58, no. 3 (2005): 245–253.

7. David F. Larcker and Brian Tayan, "Board of Directors: Duties and Liabilities," Corporate Governance Research Initiative Quick Guide Series, Stanford Graduate School of Business, 2015.

8. Richard C. Breeden, *Restoring Trust: Report to the Hon. Jed S. Rakoff, the United States District Court for the Southern District of New York on Corporate Governance for the Future of MCI, Inc.* (Brussels: European Corporate Governance Institute, 2003), https://www.ecgi.global/code/restoring-trust-breeden-report-corporate-governance-future-mci-inc.

9. B. Joseph White and William K. Hall, "Better Board Process for Better Company Results," *Directors and Boards* (2nd quarter, 2016): 21–25.

10. Christian Casal and Christian Caspar, "Building a Forward-Looking Board," *McKinsey Quarterly*, February 2014.

11. Richard D. Parsons and Marc A. Feigen, "The Boardroom's Quiet Revolution," *Harvard Business Review* 92, no. 3 (March 2014): 98–104.

12. Chinta Bhagat and Conor Kehoe, "High-Performing Boards: What's on Their Agenda?" *McKinsey Quarterly*, April 2014.

13. Committee for Economic Development, "Restoring Trust in Corporate Governance: The Six Essential Tasks of Boards of Directors and Business Leaders" (policy brief, Washington DC, January 2010).

14. See Ronald J. Gilson and Jeffrey N. Gordon, "Board 3.0: An Introduction," *Business Lawyer* 74 (Spring 2019): 351–366; and Michael Reyner and Richard Phillips, "Renaissance Directors: Reinvigorating Public Companies," MWM Consulting, 2018.

15. Michael E. Porter, "What Is Strategy?" *Harvard Business Review* 74, no. 6 (November–December 1996): 61–78.

16. For the "central idea" concept, see Ram Charan, Dennis Carey, and Michael Useem, *Boards That Lead* (Boston: Harvard Business School Publishing, 2014). For the "strategy kernel" concept, see Richard Rumelt, *Good Strategy Bad Strategy: The Difference and Why It Matters* (London: Profile Books, 2011). For the "strategic intent" concept, see Gary Hamel and C. K. Prahalad, "Strategic Intent," *Harvard Business Review* (May–June 1989): 63–76.

17. Yves Doz and Mikko Kosonen, *Fast Strategy: How Strategic Agility Will Help You Stay Ahead of the Game* (Philadelphia: Wharton School Publishing, 2008).

18. Kevin P. Hendry, Geoffrey C. Kiel, and Gavin Nicholson, "How Boards Strategise: A Strategy as Practice View," *Long Range Planning* 43 (2010): 33–56.

19. Robert A. Burgelman, Webb McKinney, and Philip E. Meza, *Becoming Hewlett Packard: Why Strategic Leadership Matters* (Oxford: Oxford University Press, 2017).

20. Roger L. Martin, "The Trouble with Directors," *The Conference Board Review* (Summer (2011): 36–39.

21. Hal Gregersen, "Bursting the CEO Bubble," *Harvard Business Review* (March–April 2017): 76–83.

22. William L. Howell, "Uncontrollable Risks and the Role of the Board of Directors" (PhD diss., University of St. Gallen, 2016).

23. David Sheppard and Guy Chazan, "Rhine Drought Leaves Europe's Industry High and Dry," *Financial Times*, October 25, 2018.

24. Rakesh Khurana, *Searching for a Corporate Savior: The Irrational Quest for Charismatic CEOs* (Princeton, NJ: Princeton University Press, 2002).

Chapter 5

1. Roger L. Martin, "Motivations for Joining a Board," *Directors and Boards* (2nd quarter, 2012): 71–72.

2. Joern Hoppmann, Florian Naegele, and Bastien Girod, "Boards as a Source of Inertia: Examining the Internal Challenges and Dynamics of Boards of Directors in Times of Environmental Discontinuities," *Academy of Management Journal* 62, no. 2 (2019): 437–468.

3. Board Appointments, "How Much Do UK Non Executive Directors Get Paid?" June 16, 2022, https://boardappointments.co.uk/uk-non-executive-director-remuneration.

4. Spencer Stuart, "2022 S&P 500 Compensation Snapshot," accessed February 27, 2023, https://www.spencerstuart.com/-/media/2022/september/compensationsnapshot/compensation_snapshot_final_9_07_22.pdf.

5. Steven Boivie, Scott D. Graffin, Abbie G. Oliver, and Michael C. Withers, "Come Aboard! Exploring the Effects of Directorships in the Executive Labor Market," *Academy of Management Journal* 59, no. 5 (2016): 1681–1706.

6. Boivie et al., "Come Aboard!"

7. The Conference Board, "CEO Succession Practices in the Russell 3000 and S&P 500: 2021 Edition," June 21, 2021.

8. Hoppmann, Naegele, and Girod, "Boards as a Source of Inertia."

9. Pekka Ala-Pietilä, interview by the authors, August 31, 2018.

10. Paul Verhaeghen, Alexandra N. Trani, and Shelley Aikman, "On Being Found: How Habitual Patterns of Thought Influence Creative Interest, Behavior, and Ability," *Creativity Research Journal* 29, no. 1 (2017): 1–9.

11. Giovanni Gavetti, "The New Psychology of Strategic Leadership," *Harvard Business Review* (July–August 2011): 118–125.

12. For more on complexity and strategy, see Ralph D. Stacey, "The Science of Complexity: An Alternative Perspective for Strategic Change Processes," *Strategic Management Journal* 16 (1995): 477–495; and Richard T. Pascale, Mark Millemann, and Linda Gioja, *Surfing the Edge of Chaos: The Laws of Nature and the New Laws of Business* (New York: Crown Publishers, 2000).

13. Martin L. Gimpl and Stephen R. Dakin, "Management and Magic," *California Management Review* (Fall 1984): 125–136.

14. Charles R. Schwenk, "Cognitive Simplification Processes in Strategic Decision Making," *Strategic Management Journal* 5, no. 2 (1984): 111–128.

15. Hans H. Hinterhuber and Wolfgang Popp, "Are You a Strategist or Just a Manager?" *Harvard Business Review* (January–February 1992): 105–113.

16. See Hal Gregersen, *Questions Are the Answer: A Breakthrough Approach to Your Most Vexing Problems at Work and in Life* (New York: HarperCollins, 2018).

17. Karl E. Weick and Kathleen M. Sutcliffe, *Managing the Unexpected* (San Francisco: Jossey-Bass, 2001).

18. Daniel Levinthal and Claus Rerup, "Crossing an Apparent Chasm: Bridging Mindful and Less-Mindful Perspectives on Organizational Learning," *Organization Science* 17, no. 4 (2006): 502–513.

19. Erica Schoenberger, "Corporate Strategy and Corporate Strategists: Power, Identity, and Knowledge within the Firm," *Environment and Planning* 26 (1994): 435–451.

20. K. Klein, "Does Gender Diversity on Boards Really Boost Company Performance?" *Knowledge@Wharton*, May 18, 2017, https://knowledge.wharton .upenn.edu/article/will-gender-diversity-boards-really-boost-company -performance/; and Stephanie J. Creary, Mary-Hunter McDonnell, Sakshi Ghai, and Jared Scruggs, "When and Why Diversity Improves Your Board's Performance," *Harvard Business Review Digital Articles*, March 27, 2019.

21. Alison Reynolds and David Lewis, "Teams Solve Problems Faster When They're More Cognitively Diverse," *Harvard Business Review Digital Articles*, March 30, 2017.

22. Chris Clearfield and Andras Tilcsik, *Meltdown: Why Our Systems Fail and What We Can Do About It* (New York: Penguin Books, 2018).

23. Razvan Lungeanu and Edward J. Zajac, "Thinking Broad and Deep: Why Some Directors Exert an Outsized Influence on Strategic Change," *Organization Science* 30, no. 3 (May–June 2019): 489–508.

24. Sureyya Burca Avci, Cindy A. Schipani, and H. Nejat Seyhun, "The Elusive Monitoring Function of Independent Directors," *University of Pennsylvania Journal of Business Law* (2019): 235–287.

25. Alexander Ljungqvist and Konrad Raff, "Busy Directors: Strategic Interaction and Monitoring Synergies," working paper 533/2017, ECGI Working Paper Series in Finance, March 2018.

26. Jon Carter, senior partner at Egon Zehnder, Palo Alto, interview by the authors, June 5, 2018.

27. Spencer Stuart, "Boardroom Best Practice," 2017, https://www.spencer stuart.com/research-and-insight/boardroom-best-practice.

28. Joann S. Lublin, "Smaller Boards Get Bigger Returns," *Wall Street Journal*, August 26, 2014.

29. In comparison, across Europe, term limits are specified in corporate governance codes and vary from four years in Sweden, Spain, and the Netherlands to six years in France (at which point directors have to be reelected if they wish to serve an additional term). In the United Kingdom, directors of FTSE 100 companies are limited to a nine-year term, though the average tenure has remained at just over four years for the decade leading to 2022. For more information on the composition of boards across Europe, see the "2023 UK Spencer Stuart Board Index" (https://www.spencerstuart.com/research -and-insight/uk-board-index/).

30. Harvard Law School Forum on Corporate Governance, "Corporate Board Practices in the Russell 3000 and S&P 500," October 18, 2020,

https://corpgov.law.harvard.edu/2020/10/18/corporate-board-practices-in-the -russell-3000-and-sp-500/.

31. Harvard Law School Forum on Corporate Governance, "Corporate Board Practices in the Russell 3000, S&P 500, and S&P Mid-Cap 400," November 6, 2021, https://corpgov.law.harvard.edu/2021/11/06/corporate-board -practices-in-the-russell-3000-sp-500-and-sp-mid-cap-400/.

32. Sydney Finkelstein, conversation with authors, February 16, 2023.

33. Yves Doz and Mikko Kosonen, *Fast Strategy: How Strategic Agility Will Help You Stay Ahead of the Game* (Philadelphia: Wharton School Publishing, 2008).

34. William B. Stevenson and Robert F. Radin, "The Minds of the Board of Directors: The Effects of Formal Position and Informal Networks among Board Members on Influence and Decision Making," *Journal of Management & Governance* (February 2014): 421–460.

35. Ian Appel, Todd A. Gormlet, and Donald B. Keim, "Standing on the Shoulders of Giants: The Effect of Passive Investors on Activism," *Review of Financial Studies* 32, no. 7 (2019): 2720–2774.

36. Annet Aris, interview by the authors, July 2018, and Pekka Ala-Pietilä, interview by the authors, August 31, 2018.

37. Ram Charan, Dennis Carey, and Michael Useem, *Boards That Lead* (Boston: Harvard Business School Publishing, 2014).

38. Jeanne Sahadi, "Should CEOs Double as Board Chairs? Increasingly S&P 500 Companies Are Saying No," *CNN Business*, October 31, 2019, https:// edition.cnn.com/2019/10/31/success/ceo-board-chair-split-role/index.html; Aman Kidwai, "The Dual CEO-Chairman Role Is Losing Favor on Public Boards," *Fortune.com*, July 15, 2022, https://fortune.com/2022/07/15/ceo-board -chairman-losing-favor-independent-director-sp500/.

39. David F. Larcker and Brian Tayan, "Chairman and CEO: The Controversy over Board Leadership Structure," working paper CGRP58, Rock Center for Corporate Governance Stanford, Closer Look Series, June 24, 2016, 1–11.

40. Sarah Gordon, "I Covered the City for 20 Years—Here's What I Learnt," *Financial Times*, March 8, 2019.

41. Timothy J. Quigley and Donald C. Hambrick, "When the Former CEO Stays On as Board Chair: Effects on Successor Discretion, Strategic Change, and Performance," *Strategic Management Journal* 33 (2012): 834–859.

42. Alison Gaines, interview by the authors, August 7, 2018.

43. Hoppmann, Naegele, and Girod, "Boards as a Source of Inertia."

Chapter 6

1. Chinta Bhagat, Martin Hirt, and Conor Kehoe, "Tapping the Strategic Potential of Boards," *McKinsey Quarterly*, February 2013.

2. Liselotte Engstam, Mats Magnusson, Ludo Van der Heyden, and Magnus Karlsson, "Innovation and Corporate Renewal Also Disrupt Boards," *MGMT of Innovation and Technology*, accessed August 18, 2019, https://mgmt .imit.se/artiklar/innovation-and-corporate-renewal-also-disrupt-boards/.

3. Rand Corporation, "Delphi Method," accessed October 15, 2019, https:// www.rand.org/topics/delphi-method.html.

4. Michel Godet and Febrice Roubelat, "Creating the Future: The Use and Misuse of Scenarios," *Long Range Planning* 29, no. 2 (1996): 164–171.

5. For the full story and analysis of why the two Baby Bell companies, both spinoffs of AT&T, fared so differently in their ability to embrace a disruptive technology and build a wireless business, given that they began life with similar strategies, assets, and markets, see Tomo Noda and Joseph L. Bower, "Strategy Making as Iterated Processes of Resource Allocation," *Strategic Management Journal* 17 (1996): 159–192.

6. Ken English, interview by the authors, September 27, 2004.

Chapter 7

1. Mikko Kosonen and Yves Doz, "How Good Is Strategy Making in the Company You Oversee? And How You Can Improve It!" *Boardview* 1 (2013).

2. For more detail about Nokia, see Yves Doz and Keeley Wilson, *Ringtone: Exploring the Rise and Fall of Nokia in Mobile Phones* (Oxford: Oxford University Press, 2015).

3. Yves Doz and Andrea Cuomo, "Corporate Governance 4.0: Facing Interdependency and Speed in a Complex World," INSEAD Working Paper 2017/45/STR, July 2017.

4. All subsequent quotes from Catmull are from Ed Catmull with Amy Wallace, *Creativity, Inc.: Overcoming the Unseen Forces That Stand in the Way of True Inspiration* (London: Transworld Publishers, 2014).

5. Mary Yoko Brannen and Yves L. Doz, "Corporate Languages and Strategic Agility: Trapped in Your Jargon or Lost in Translation?" *California Management Review* 54, no. 3 (2012): 77–97.

Chapter 8

1. Lisa Farwell and Ruth Wohlwend-Lloyd, "Narcissistic Processes: Optimistic Expectations, Favorable Self-Evaluations, and Self-Enhancing Attributions," *Journal of Personality* 66 (1998): 65–83.

2. Arijit Chatterjee and Timothy G. Pollock, "Master of Puppets: How Narcissistic CEOs Construct Their Professional Worlds," *Academy of Management Review* 42, no. 4 (2017): 703–725.

3. Arijit Chatterjee and Donald C. Hambrick, "It's All about Me: Narcissistic CEOs and Their Effects on Company Strategy and Performance," *Administrative Science Quarterly* 52 (2007): 351–386.

4. Robert A. Burgelman, Webb McKinney, and Philip E. Meza, *Becoming Hewlett Packard: Why Strategic Leadership Matters* (Oxford: Oxford University Press, 2017).

5. Chris Morris, "Disney CEO Bob Iger Speaks Out about Replacing Bob Chapek Fresh Off a Major Restructure Announcement Saying He 'Created a Huge Divide,'" *Fortune.com*, February 9, 2023, https://fortune.com/2023/02/09/disney-ceo-bob-iger-speaks-out-bob-chapek-created-a-huge-divide/.

6. Claudio Fernández-Aráoz, "21st Century Talent Spotting: Why Potential Now Trumps Brains, Experience, and 'Competencies,'" *Harvard Business Review* (June 2014): 46–56.

7. For a deeper discussion on the phenomenon and dangers of superstar leaders, we recommend an excellent book by Rakesh Khurana, *Searching for a Corporate Savior: The Irrational Quest for Charismatic CEOs* (Princeton, NJ: Princeton University Press, 2002).

8. Claudio Fernández-Aráoz, "Why Boards Get C-Suite Succession So Wrong," *Harvard Business Review Digital Articles*, May 15, 2015.

9. Elena Lytkina Botelho, Kim Rosenkoetter Powell, Stephen Kincaid, and Dina Wang, "What Sets Successful CEOs Apart: The Four Essential Behaviors That Help Them Win the Top Job and Thrive Once They Get It," *Harvard Business Review* (May–June 2017): 70–77.

10. Matthew Bidwell, "Paying More to Get Less: Specific Skills, Matching and the Effects of External Hiring versus Internal Promotion," *Administrative Science Quarterly* 56, no. 3 (2011): 369–407.

11. Harvard Law School Forum on Corporate Governance, "CEO Succession Practices in the Russell 3000 and S&P 500: 2022 Edition," September 19, 2022, https://corpgov.law.harvard.edu/2022/09/19/ceo-succession-practices-in-the-russell-3000-and-sp-500-2022-edition/.

12. Joseph L. Bower, *The CEO Within: Why Inside Outsiders Are the Key to Succession Planning* (Boston: Harvard Business School Press, 2007).

13. Rajeev Kohli and Alonso Martinez, "Finding Coherence in Diversified Conglomerates: How Tata and 3M Pursue Strategic Growth," Columbia Business School, Case ID 170503, October 2016.

Chapter 9

1. For a more detailed discussion of the defining characteristics of strategic assets, see Jay Barney, "Firm Resources and Sustained Competitive Advantage," *Journal of Management* 17, no. 1 (1991): 99–120; Ingemar Dierickx and Karel Cool, "Asset Stock Accumulation and Sustainability of Competitive Advantage," *Management Science* 35, no. 12 (December 1989): 1504–1511.

2. Todd Zenger, "What Is the Theory of Your Firm?" *Harvard Business Review* (June 2013): 73–78.

3. Lev Baruch, "Ending the Accounting-for-Intangibles Status Quo," *European Accounting Review* 28, no. 4 (2019): 713–736.

4. Daniel McCarthy and Peter Fader, "How to Value a Company by Analyzing Its Customers," *Harvard Business Review* (January–February 2020): 51–55.

5. Yves Doz and Keeley Wilson, *Ringtone: Exploring the Rise and Fall of Nokia in Mobile Phones* (Oxford: Oxford University Press, 2015).

6. Henk Akkermans and Luk N. Van Wassenhove, "Supply Chain Tsunamis: Research on Low-Probability, High-Impact Disruptions," *Journal of Supply Chain Management* 54, no. 1 (2018): 64–76.

7. Susan Lund, James Manyika, Jonathan Woetzel, Edward Barriball, Mekala Krishnan, Knut Alicke, Michael Birshan, et al., "Risk, Resilience, and Rebalancing in Global Value Chains," *McKinsey Global Institute*, August 2020.

8. For more on dynamic capabilities, see David J. Teece and Gary Pisano, "The Dynamic Capabilities of Firms: An Introduction," *Corporate Change* 3, no. 3 (1994): 537–556; Kathleen M. Eisenhardt and Jeffrey A. Martin, "Dynamic Capabilities: What Are They?" *Strategic Management Journal* 21 (2000): 1105–1121; Constance E. Helfat and Margaret A. Peteraf, "Managerial Cognitive Capabilities and the Microfoundations of Dynamic Capabilities," *Strategic Management Journal* 36, no. 6 (2015): 831–850; and Charles A. O'Reilly and Michael L. Tushman, "Ambidexterity as a Dynamic Capability: Resolving the Innovator's Dilemma," *Research in Organizational Behavior* 28 (2008): 185–206.

9. Clay Chandler, "Ping An's Castle Made of Data," *Fortune*, August 2019.

Chapter 10

1. Jeffrey Pfeffer and Robert I. Sutton, *The Knowing-Doing Gap: How Smart Companies Turn Knowledge into Action* (Boston: Harvard Business School Press, 2000).

2. Gartner, "Invest Implications: 'Magic Quadrant for Cloud Infrastructure as a Service,'" August 23, 2013, https://www.gartner.com/en/documents/2578615.

Chapter 11

1. International Labour Organization, "Why Would Labour Productivity Surge during a Pandemic?" December 14, 2021, https://ilostat.ilo.org/why-would-labour-productivity-surge-during-a-pandemic/.

2. Joseph B. Fuller and William R. Kerr, "The Great Resignation Didn't Start with the Pandemic," *Harvard Business Review Digital Articles*, March 23, 2022.

3. Thomas W. Britt, "Black Hawk Down at Work," *Harvard Business Review* (January 2003): 16–17.

4. Patrick Butler, interview with the authors, April 4, 2023.

5. Charles A. O'Reilly and Jeffrey Pfeffer, *Hidden Value: How Great Companies Achieve Extraordinary Results with Ordinary People* (Boston: Harvard Business School Press, 2000).

6. Andrew S. Grove, *Only the Paranoid Survive: How to Exploit the Crisis Points That Challenge Every Company and Career* (New York: Currency Doubleday, 1996).

7. Gilad Chen, Bradley L. Kirkman, Ruth Kanfer, Don Allen, and Benson Rosen, "A Multilevel Study of Leadership, Empowerment, and Performance in Teams," *Journal of Applied Psychology* 92, no. 2 (2007): 331–346.

8. Rob Cross, Wayne Baker, and Andrew Parker, "What Creates Energy in Organizations?" *MIT Sloan Management Review* 44 (2003): 51–56.

9. Albert Bandura, "Self-Efficacy: Toward a Unifying Theory of Behavioral Change," *Psychological Review* 84 (1977): 191–215. For a deeper dive, also see Albert Bandura, *Self-Efficacy in Changing Societies* (Cambridge: Cambridge University Press, 1995).

10. Cristina B. Gibson and P. Christopher Earley, "Collective Cognition in Action: Accumulation, Interaction, Examination, and Accommodation in the Development and Operation of Group Efficacy Beliefs in the Workplace," *Academy of Management Review* 32, no. 2 (2007): 438–458.

Some Final Thoughts

1. International Monetary Fund, "World Economic Outlook Update: Inflation Peaking amid Low Growth," January 2023, https://www.imf.org/en/Publications/WEO/Issues/2023/01/31/world-economic-outlook-update-january-2023.

2. World Health Organization, "Air Pollution," accessed October 28, 2021, https://www.who.int/airpollution/en/, and "New WHO Global Air Quality Guidelines Aim to Save Millions of Lives from Air Pollution," September 22, 2021, https://www.who.int/news/item/22-09-2021-new-who-global-air-quality-guidelines-aim-to-save-millions-of-lives-from-air-pollution.

3. The documentary is available to view on Apple TV (https://tv.apple.com/us/movie/the-year-earth-changed/umc.cmc.3fob3t7nfhehpb3ilgynzxmnu).

4. World Economic Forum, *The Global Risks Report 2022*, 17th ed. (Geneva: World Economic Forum, 2022), https://www3.weforum.org/docs/WEF_The_Global_Risks_Report_2022.pdf.

5. United Nations Department of Economic and Social Affairs, "Growing at a Slower Pace, World Population Is Expected to Reach 9.7 Billion in 2050 and Could Peak at Nearly 11 Billion around 2100," June 17, 2019, https://www.un.org/development/desa/en/news/population/world-population-prospects-2019.html.

Acknowledgments

As is so often the case, the contributions of many different people helped shape our thoughts, sharpen our arguments, and improve our work. First and foremost, we owe a debt of gratitude to Andrea Cuomo for the critical role he played in the early stage of our research: developing ideas with us, being an intellectual sparring partner, and always providing energy and enthusiasm to spur us on. We are grateful to old and trusted friends: Mikko Kosonen, for the work we did together researching boards and strategy, and Steven Veldhoen, for providing honest critiques and helpful suggestions as we were developing our arguments. Thanks are also owed to Filipe Morais, Jose Santos, Olli Lauren, Ludo Van der Heyden, and the anonymous reviewers who provided invaluable feedback to help us improve the book. Ludo again comes in for thanks, along with Muriel Larvaron, for inviting us to INSEAD's Corporate Governance Initiative events, where we had the opportunity to meet hundreds of board directors from around the world who were willing to share their experience with us, for which we are immensely grateful. Over the course of our research, we interviewed a great many people and although it is impossible to list everyone individually, we thank each and every one of you for your time and insights. We would like to acknowledge Neal Maillet, our editor at Berrett-Koehler, for his encouragement and patience. And, last but not least, our work would not have been possible without funding from INSEAD, and for this, we appreciate the support of Laurence Capron, Timothy van Zandt, Javier Gimeno, Ziv Carmon, and Lily Fang.

Even though so many people have made valuable contributions to this book, any errors, misinterpretations, and shortcomings remain our own.

Yves and Keeley have worked together at INSEAD for over two decades, researching and writing on a broad range of strategy-related issues, from strengthening key capabilities in governance to the strategy process, innovation, strategic alliances, complexity, and managing change. Their consulting and advisory work has helped senior executives across a wide range of industries around the world, including Airbus, Avery Dennison, BHP, GSK, IBM, Intel, Microsoft, P&G, Reuters, Schneider, Shell, Teva, Toyota, and Xerox. They have published numerous books and articles together, including *Ringtone: Exploring the Rise and Fall of Nokia in Mobile Phones*, which won the Academy of Management's best management book award in 2018, and "10 Rules for Managing Global Innovation," which was selected by *Harvard Business Review* as a definitive article for the best-selling HBR's 10 Must Reads series.

Yves Doz comes from an academic background. He has taught at Harvard Business School and Stanford Graduate School of Business in the United States and at leading business schools in Europe and Asia. He is currently the Solvay Chaired Professor of Technological Innovation, Emeritus, at INSEAD. His academic peers elected him a fellow of all three major academic societies in management, one of only four scholars worldwide to be bestowed such recognition. He was the first recipient of the CK Prahalad Scholar-Practitioner Award from the Strategic Management Society for bringing research findings to management practice, and he is a holder of a Lifetime Distinguished Scholar Award from the Academy of Management.

Keeley Wilson comes from a research and consulting background. Both in her work with Strategos and as a senior research fellow at INSEAD, she has focused on translating the innovative concepts and theories she develops into practical tools to help leaders navigate the challenges they face. She has been widely praised for her ability to articulate complex ideas clearly and concisely. She has lived and worked in Europe and Asia and is currently an independent coach and consultant.

Dear reader,

Thank you for picking up this book and welcome to the worldwide BK community! You're joining a special group of people who have come together to create positive change in their lives, organizations, and communities.

What's BK all about?

Our mission is to connect people and ideas to create a world that works for all.

Why? Our communities, organizations, and lives get bogged down by old paradigms of self-interest, exclusion, hierarchy, and privilege. But we believe that can change. That's why we seek the leading experts on these challenges—and share their actionable ideas with you.

A welcome gift

To help you get started, we'd like to offer you a **free copy** of one of our bestselling ebooks:

www.bkconnection.com/welcome

When you claim your **free ebook**, you'll also be subscribed to our blog.

Our freshest insights

Access the best new tools and ideas for leaders at all levels on our blog at ideas.bkconnection.com.

Sincerely,

Your friends at Berrett-Koehler